HAPPIER
AS A
WOMAN

HAPPIER AS A WOMAN

TRANSFORMING FRIENDSHIPS, TRANSFORMING LIVES

MARTINA GISELLE RAMIREZ
&
ALICIA PARTNOY

CLEiS
PRESS

Published in the United States by Cleis Press, an imprint of Start Midnight, LLC, 101 Hudson Street, Thirty-Seventh Floor, Suite 3705, Jersey City, NJ 07302.

Printed in the United States.
Cover photos: Martina Giselle Ramirez, iStock
Cover design: Allyson Fields
Text design: Frank Wiedemann
First Edition.
10 9 8 7 6 5 4 3 2 1

Trade paper ISBN: 978-1-62778-238-8
E-book ISBN: 978-1-62778-239-5

Some names and identifying details have been changed to protect the privacy of certain individuals.

Acknowledgments

· ·

We would like to thank Loyola Marymount University's BCLA Faculty Research and Writing Grant and the Rains Research Assistant Funds Program for providing the support for this project, and Hannah Bennett and Mindy Waizer for their careful editing hands.Our deep gratitude goes to Juliana Zapata Acosta, Morgan Mostrom, Alejandra Loperena Molina, Marissa Cheng, Juliana Kodama, and Haley Smith, our amazing research assistants, who helped us transcribe and edit many hours of conversations and set up the scanner to produce high-quality pictures for the manuscript. Without them, this book would never have been finished on time.

To María Eva Rossi and Christine Jorgensen.
Your courage inspires us.
The world misses your presence.

Contents

Weaving Solidarities

Alicia Partnoy

Alicia and Martina signing the book contract with Cleis Press, with Martina's former student Stephanie Kawecki as witness, September 2016

Welcome to our lives and our struggles, dear reader. In these pages Dr. Martina Ramirez, a transgender professor of biology, will share her journey from her childhood in a poor and conservative Mexican American family to her current life as, finally, a happy woman. Through personal accounts, photos, reflections, testimonies, and hours of conversations, you will learn about her experiences as a Latina enduring multilayered discrimination but finding the strength to survive and work for social justice. As an ally in her journey, I lend my hand and heart to weave this tapestry of solidarity which aims to inspire those who struggle for the world to accept, understand, and embrace their real gender identity. Ours is a labor of education, an effort to open eyes and minds, to fight against hatred and indifference.

Let me tell you about the seeds of our friendship and this book. In 2014, after Martina helped me translate a spider-related word in one of my short stories into English, I half-jokingly wrote in an email to her that we should coteach a class on "Spiders in/and Literature." Her enthusiastic response came right back, and soon after we were at work on the class proposal. It was approved. That fall semester we met our thirty-nine students. There was some shifting in the registration records when a few of them dropped the course after meeting the Spider Lab queen tarantula named Fluffy, whom Martina brought to the first day of class to welcome the freshly minted college students. The semester was intense, at times stressful, at times exhilarating, but it made clear to me that collaborating with Martina was a seamless process.

Two years later, in April 2016, I was invited to give a TEDx Youth Talk in San Diego. There, I met Dr. Eli Green. His talk, "A Toolkit for Becoming a Transgender Ally,"[1] inspired me to ask Martina if she wanted to write a book together.

"I'm game," she smiled with excitement. "Lately people have been telling me that my life is very interesting: a transgender Latina, adopted as a baby, raised in a poor family, someone who attended college and got a doctoral. They ask me to write a book, but I don't have the time."

She did, however, make time to sit for hours of recorded talks, to sift through memories and photographs, and even to build a mysterious (to me) device powerful enough to digitize her childhood color slides. Through that experience we became friends, and I have had the privilege of accompanying her on the recent steps of her journey, including her gender-confirming surgery in December 2016.

While I was weaving solidarities with Martina Ramirez, our lives felt connected in uncanny ways. I still remember her beaming selfie on Facebook. She was holding an index card with the date for her surgery:

Martina's Facebook photo announcing the date of her gender-confirming surgery, June 2016

December 22, 2016. Underneath, she had written, "So it will be a very special Xmas, before coming home on Jan 1, 2017 as a very happy woman ☺☺☺."

I had also gained my freedom around that time of the year," I added to the more than one hundred post likes and well-wishing messages. Later, in my office crowded with books about my own life as a former political prisoner in Argentina, I told her that on December 22, back in 1979, I had arrived in the US as a refugee.

My story was, I believe, the fifth book published by Cleis Press, the same company that puts this book in your hands today. Back in 1986, Cleis, the brainchild of Felice Newman and Frederique Delacoste, was one of two feminist presses in the United States. The visionary couple conceived this women's press with a strong focus on lesbian writings. In a wonderful act of solidarity, while their publishing house grew to issue over five hundred LGBTQ+ titles, they kept my book, *The Little School: Tales of Disappearance and Survival,* alive for almost forty years. In the meantime, justice has been achieved in Argentina, where my vignettes about life in a concentration camp were finally published in 2006. The book was used as evidence in the trials against the genocide perpetrators. People realized that we, the victims and survivors, were not terrorist monsters as the dictatorship had claimed; we had been fighting for social justice.

Martina has also undertaken a labor of education for social justice. Through her teaching, mentoring, courageous transition, and telling of her own experience, she seeks to inspire young people to follow their dreams, to be true to themselves and, she says, "to learn that we are not monsters." She reminds us that "sometimes what the media reports about transgender celebrities is not helpful. See, most of us are just regular people."

Martina's journey and her life story need to be told today. "If you look at people who are transgender and you look at the statistics, you realize the numbers of us who drift into depression and into suicide is pretty high," she said. "I knew by 2010 that if I did not do something, I was going to find myself drifting down hill, and I did not want to go there."

Martina's journey aims to give hope to the many marginalized people who struggle for recognition of their gender identity. "Being this way, as I am now, is so much like coming home," Martina tells the world. She finds joy in the opportunity to help others be happier.

Martina's Childhood and Policed Gender Behavior

Martina Giselle Ramirez and Alicia Partnoy
August 3, 2016

A: In her book *Redefining Realness*, transgender rights activist Janet Mock wrote that her femininity was heavily policed by her father when she was a child.[2] He kept asking her not to act like a sissy, but he would also tell her that he loved her. He was pretty expressive and demonstrative, unlike your father. Do you remember if you ever allowed yourself to display any characteristics of your true gender as a child? Was there anything that gave your parents a clue?

M: Because my dad was a former military man, there was no space in that household for anything but "males behave this way, females do this." I respected my father and admired his example of dealing with adversity, but in terms of sharing personal stuff with him, it was really rare. It bothered me that I went through high school never dating anybody, but of course my parent's view of such things was, "If you date people, you're not serious. You need to be focused on academics because we are poor people and you are our path to success in life."

My parents really invested all their energy into me. Given that their lives had been destroyed by racism, they looked at anything that was less than hard work as if you were just playing. I remember at some point having a conversation with my father where I hinted that I was feeling bad, and it didn't really go down very well with him.

A: Did you tell him about not dating, about their standards?

M: It was about feeling that it would have been nice to have some social life as opposed to just doing schoolwork all the time.

A: What did he say?

M: I don't remember. I know that what he said wasn't very pleasant. I was like this little turtle, sticking my head out briefly and getting bashed, so then I just pulled back in. That's the way he was. I could never have a conversation with him about serious stuff.

A: And with your mother?

M: My mom was more people-oriented than my dad. We got along in that regard, but at the end of the day I knew she believed a lot of the same things that he did. I didn't agree with him about his attitude toward different races, since he had issues with Asian Americans, African Americans, Anglos, Jews, and even Latinos. The only people he considered respectable were Mexicans like himself, who had been in this country for a long time, and so he even despised the newly arrived from Mexico. I would sometimes challenge him on these ideas, and I would get hit for speaking back to him if he was sufficiently annoyed.

A: He slapped you?

M: Oh yes. He slapped me.

A: The belt?

M: Yes, I got that too when I was a kid, I got the belt, of course.

A: What did you do to "deserve" being hit with his belt? What kind of things?

M: For example, I would just tell him to his face, "Look, you go to church on Sundays. You hear about how Jesus is hanging out with everybody. Do you see him ranking people? Do you see Jesus doing that?" See, his family and my mom's family had come over during the revolution in Mexico in the 1920s. They migrated around the US, doing agricultural work, picking fruit. At some point both families came to Pomona. They were in a segregated city where it was illegal to speak Spanish in the classroom. Even the Catholic Church in town was segregated: there was the one for whites, and the one for brown people. My father's view was that the people who came over when our family did, in the 1920s, were really awesome, but here were these people from Mexico who had been here for five, ten years or less. They played loud music, they did this and that. For my father they were less than us.

A: How old were you?

M: I was in high school or younger. I just couldn't keep my mouth shut with stuff like that since I thought it was so stupid. Here's an African American person walking by . . . boom! Some comment comes out of his mouth. Many times, I would just say something right there and he would get mad, slap me, do whatever.

A: And that's how he was physically abusive?

M: Oh, yes!

A: But it's weird because he suffered extreme discrimination, too. His whole life was destroyed by racism. And then he would still be racist.

M: Indeed! Somehow I had enough wherewithal to speak up, because he was an intimidating guy. I might have just played it safe and said nothing, but I couldn't.

A: Sometimes it got to be too much.

M: Yes, this was stupid. Does it matter who I'm playing with? There was an African American girl in an elementary school class who was really pretty and I liked her. But would I ever tell my dad that I was attracted to this African American Woman? No way!

A: Why did you like her? How old were you?

M: I was in seventh or eighth grade probably. She was the little sister of a friend, and she was really chill. I sat in class behind her for a whole year. We became friends. But see, for me, the relationship thing has always been about what's in your soul. What kind of goodness are you bringing to the world? The packaging didn't matter a lot to me. Over my life I have dated people that were plus-size, people that were thin, people of different ethnicities, not that I dated a lot. I also knew to some extent that physical beauty fades. What stays is your inner light, whatever it is, and you better get that right when you pick somebody, since that's the thing that is going to last.

Walking My Talk, Inspiring Students

Martina Giselle Ramirez, July 29, 2016

I find myself telling my students semester after semester: "If you become a scientist, or a doctor, for example, you are going to be in a world where you will see unjust things done and people treated less than appropriately for a variety of reasons. And you, on the other hand, are going to be a person with nice degree and letters behind your name. You are going to become a person of authority in your world, with a chance to make changes in your workplace, to mentor people. That is how you act as a star in the darkness."

I think they get my message. For me, this professor role is not just about teaching them skills, science, statistics, or how to present their findings at a conference. It is about teaching values and ways to approach the world from a different perspective. I try to model a way of being a professional that is perhaps different from what they might expect professors to be like. I usually get to know my students really well. I get invited to their graduation parties, to their weddings.

There are two images that work together for me: the one I mentioned of being a star in the darkness, and another one inspired by *Star Trek*. You might remember that one of the goals of the Starship Enterprise was to enter into the trajectory of various worlds. There's a foundational vision as to what this spacecraft and its crew are going to do as they go through their adventures. Once in any new world, I just tell my students, whatever you think is your prime directive—follow it. I tell them that for me, my prime directive is to always do what you can to help others, especially those who are at the margins in terms of access and opportunities. I've always had that mission driving me. That's why I never became dysfunctional, even when I could not be totally open about who I was. For me, it has been a saving grace to have this bigger purpose.

The difference now—according to people who have known me for a long time, from before I became openly transgender at Loyola Marymount University—is that I have become even more of an example because people can see the sacrifices I made to step away from how I was living my life before. They can see an example of being true to your vision of life. Too often we see examples of people playing it safe because, "Oh, I have so much invested in this and that," or "I'm older—why complicate my life? I'll just suck it up and deal with it."

I don't belittle people who think like that. I tell students that, obviously, it is a choice you have to make. But I always tell them, "Whenever you're doing anything in life, you must find that little flame burning, like in a water heater. There has to be some excitement, some value, something that inspires you to go to work every day. But you're going to notice sometimes that the vitality of that flame is getting weaker. Then at some point it goes out, and you find yourself just going with the trajectory of your life. You have a choice at that point. You may have years invested in living a certain way, being in a relationship, being in a job situation. You can choose to compromise and hold your nose and find other outlets to be happy, or you can explore stepping away from the life you have and into a new one."

I like to tell my students about when I was a graduate school teaching assistant for a professor at The University of California, Santa Cruz. He had been a medical doctor for a number of years but stepped away when he was forty-something to return to graduate school. He got a PhD and worked with whales and dolphins doing diving physiology. He told me, "At some point, at least with my experience in medicine, I found myself thinking like I was working at an auto shop. 'Wheel them in, wheel them out.' I saw the same thing every day, I felt like there wasn't any creativity in it." That was his reality. So when the excitement or creativity went out, he started searching for something different to do, and achieved big success in a very different world.

At UC Santa Cruz, I was also a teaching assistant for a biologist who had done research with primates at Harvard. He had been a well-known primate geneticist. At some point, he walked away to enroll in an MD program at Stanford. He was teaching part time when I met him in Santa Cruz. He had this track record at Harvard, with his papers being cited all over the place, and he walked away from it all because he felt called to work with people. Everybody was shocked.

My point is that both professors were not twenty-somethings when they did this. They had families. But they were being bold. I always tell students: not everybody has the resources or the courage to do that, but if at some point you realize your little flame in life is withering down or becoming dim, then it's time to think about an avenue to go to another area that gives you some happiness.

Like those professors, I also changed avenues when I was older. I had been living as a man for many years and I was unhappy. My partner did not support my transition that much, but I went ahead with it. And that has greatly improved the way many people think of me. Before, I used to preach: "You need to find your dreams in whatever way, shape, or form they take. And if that means what you had been doing no longer makes sense, ideally you want to change your path." Not that it is easy, especially when you are middle-aged or older. Now, people see that I'm actually walking my talk, and they respect me for it.

They Finally Told Me I Was Adopted

Martina Giselle Ramirez and Alicia Partnoy
August 3, 2016

M: I don't know my biological family, though I'm really curious about them.

A: We both have to travel to Puerto Rico to find out more [*laughs*].

M: I have some clues because I went to St. Anne's Maternity Home from where I was adopted at the age of nine months. The records are actually still there, but my parents didn't tell me that I was adopted until my senior year at Loyola Marymount University. I always thought it was strange that my dad and mom got married in 1942, he went to World War II, he came back in 1946, and then years went by before I appeared on the scene in 1959. It was strange for me.

A: How old was your mom back then?

M: She was born in 1922, so in her twenties.

A: Right, she was at an age where she could have had babies.

M: The reality was that my dad was infertile. I just thought it was strange because when most of the World War II generation soldiers came back, there was a baby boom. It was like, "Let's make love because the war is over! Let us celebrate! Let's make babies!" I wondered how come my parents didn't do that. When they told me years later, it kind of made sense. "Oh yeah, I'm adopted."

A: So your parents had eleven or twelve siblings each?

M: I have loads of uncles and aunts everywhere [*laughs*].

A: A humongous family.

M: Yes, in my adoptive family I have billions of cousins [*laughs*]. You go to weddings, you go to funerals, and it's like, "Wait, who do you belong to? Where are you in the big organizational chart?" My parent's story as to why they waited so long to have a child of their own was that they were helping some of my uncles and aunts with the raising of their own kids. When they finally told me, "We actually adopted you," I was like, "Oh. I now see why they got married in 1942 and then all of a sudden I appeared seventeen years later."

A: They waited so long to tell you.

M: It was an embarrassing thing for them. That's why
    they never told me. And I think they decided to tell me
    because I was dating Rose, the person who became
    my wife.

A: They wanted to make sure she was not related to you
    [*laughs*]. Was she also Puerto Rican?

M: No, she is also Mexican American. You see, I was
    ready to leave for graduate school, I was going to
    move away. They thought they should finally tell me
    what had really happened. So I wasn't surprised.

A: You knew, somehow.

M: I just thought it was strange.

My Father: A Life Destroyed by Racism

Martina Giselle Ramirez, August 3, 2016

Helen and Martin Ramirez at a family event in
June 1981

My father was Martin John Ramirez. I have seen his pictures from World War II, and he looks *muy guapo*. I can see why my mom took notice of this guy!

The story of his life is the origin of many things that motivate me. Let me explain. My mom and dad grew up in Pomona, California. Their families had come over during the revolution in Mexico when—if you were Catholic—it wasn't very safe.

One of my parents was born in Mexico and had come over as a baby, while the other was born a few weeks after the family arrived into the US. Their families were migrant farm workers who moved to the Midwest, and then at some point came to California. They were in the Central Valley, following the harvest. Later, both families ended up with eleven and twelve kids, so they stopped wandering around, and settled in Pomona, which is an hour from Los Angeles.

This was during the Great Depression, and the oldest kids used to get jobs as soon as they were able to work. My mom and dad never finished high school because they had to work to support their families. They married in 1942. World War II was on, so my dad went off to the war. Even though he hadn't finished high school, when he came back in 1946 he was able to get a real estate license in California, as well as a permit to sell life insurance. He sold homes for forty years.

During the 1950s my dad was doing pretty well. He and my mom eventually owned three homes in town, and it was around this time that they adopted me. My dad was planning to retire about ten years later. For somebody who grew up with nothing, he was doing really well.

However, he was operating in a segregated city. Pomona was heavily segregated, and you could not live in certain parts of town if you were brown. There were housing covenants that enforced this pretty common reality back then in southern California.

There was a history here of people trying to break the covenants, trying to integrate neighborhoods, and apparently my dad started doing that. He wanted to make a living, but he was also bothered by the segregation situation.

Within a year or two of adopting me, my dad became the campaign manager for a Latino dentist who was running for city council. For decades, the Pomona city council had been run by white men. The dentist did not win, but it was pretty notable that he didn't do too badly either. People in power were concerned about this Ramirez guy who was really good at dealing with people and getting them together. So, I have been told, he was framed for embezzlement. He was targeted for elimination because he was a threat to the way things were.

My dad was convicted and went to jail. This was in 1960 or 1961, when I was a toddler.

Because he was convicted, my father lost both of his licenses. He lost the houses that he had. When he came out of jail, he was reduced to zero. The chance to make money the way he knew was all gone. He started picking citrus fruits—that's what you did in the foothills of the San Gabriel mountains. Seventy or eighty years ago, there were just miles and miles of orange and lemon groves there. So, he did that for a while.

There was never any history of alcoholism in either my mom's or my dad's families, but my dad was bitter, so he started drinking. At some point, he hit someone with his car when he was drunk and fled the scene. He got caught and was then incarcerated a second time. I remember going to visit my dad on Saturdays, but because I was underage I couldn't go inside the jail to see him. It was my mom who could. My dad never wanted her to have a driver's license, so an uncle or somebody else would drive us. He must have spent about one year in jail. I remember that we were back together watching the moon landing on TV, in July of 1969.

When he got out the second time, my dad joined Alcoholics Anonymous and he never drank again. Then he did what he had to do: he got his real estate license back, and he tried to get back on track. For a while, he was driving a donation truck for a Goodwill-type organization, Disabled American Veterans. They had secondhand stores, and I remember helping him in the summers. He would drive the truck and I would be in the back. People would leave bags of goods on the curb that they were giving away, and I would jump off the truck to get them.

The other thing that my father did was clean. There was a Disabled American Veteran thrift store in town, and my mom, my dad, and I would go and clean the store on the weekends. We had to take out all the racks for all the clothes, push them to the side, and wax the floors. I helped with that when I was about ten years old.

When he recovered his real estate license, my father tried to get back into the business world, but he had lost many years of productivity. His contemporaries had nice homes and nice cars, and my dad was starting from nothing. People talk about the effects of racism and what it does to families and, for me, that was all very personal.

My life was completely different. I adapted to living in a car for a little bit, and living in an uncle's garage for a while, before we got into low-grade rental units.

When they adopted me, my parents were very optimistic. They were in a good place. There are pictures of me as a toddler walking in the yard of one of their houses. But it didn't take very long before it all ended. It was clear that he faced discrimination because he was Mexican American.

You could even see racism in the church. There were two major Catholic churches in Pomona back then. One was the big church on Mission Boulevard. It was huge and had beautiful marble. And then there was Sacred Heart Church in the southern part of town. If you were Mexican American, that was where you would go. Both my grandfathers helped build that church. It was basically constructed with rocks taken out of rivers and streams.

Eventually in the 1970s, when I was an altar person there, the church got enough money to build a nice, new building. They still use the old church as a community center. But in the old days, you did not step into the big church on Mission Boulevard unless you were white. It was pretty clear that the message to us was, "Don't even bother, don't even try."

When people think of racism in the US, they tend to just think of black and white. Here in California, especially in southern California, you had that dynamic playing out with Mexican Americans. For me, the whole idea of treating others differently because of who they are was never theoretical. It was very real in my case.

Martina at one year old, March 1960

I Prayed and Worked Hard

Martina Giselle Ramirez and Alicia Partnoy
August 3, 2016

M: I'm very stubborn. When I started going to a mostly white and affluent high school, I decided I was not going to become a casualty. They destroyed my dad's life. I wasn't going to be next. So I prayed and I worked hard.

A: Did you fly a little under the radar with your activism? Were you scared?

M: No, no, no. See, for me I just wondered, "Why don't we have somebody who's brown as valedictorian? Why don't we have somebody brown in student government?" When I didn't see it, I thought, "Why not try?" That was my attitude. Younger students from my elementary school would come to visit this school, and they would just see a bunch of rich white kids. And if they looked at the honor roll or who was on the newspaper staff, they would rarely see people who looked like us there. So I thought we weren't really sending a good message. That was my avenue to change people's thinking. My goal was to try to help people coming to the school after me, so that they would see that if you're willing to work hard, there's no reason you can't do something. I just didn't buy into the nonsense that if you were Mexican American you were supposed to be doing menial jobs. It wasn't fair.

A: You saw that example in your father too. He did the menial jobs when nothing else was available, and after that he would try to go in another direction.

M: Yes. But we disagreed about a whole lot of stuff. He kind of had an ego.

A: Right. You never told your father about you transitioning.

M: Well, he passed away in 2007.

A: But he never had a clue about anything. Was that because you were afraid of his discipline?

M: I learned very early that sharing personal things with him was not safe. He had been a master sergeant in the US Army Corps of Engineers. People wonder where my organization comes from. I had to be that way with him. There was a place for everything, and everything was in its place. In other words, my life was like basic training. I always wondered, "Was I naturally that way, or did I learn it from growing up with a sergeant?" He made it very clear to me that showing any emotion or uncertainty about anything was unacceptable. So I didn't go there. And I knew there was no way my conservative Republican, Catholic, ex-military father was going to have anything good to say about my gender identity. Make no mistake, my dad and I went at it. For whatever reason, I did not always keep my mouth shut all the time with him. I got hit because of that. My mom had a hard time too. I felt bad for her because he didn't treat her well all the time. But if you're Mexican American and you're married in the Catholic Church, you stay with your man forever, even if he isn't the easiest person to get along with.

A: So both your mom and your dad had eleven siblings?

M: My dad. On his side there were nine guys and three girls. Most of them have passed away. Most of his brothers didn't like each other much. They were ego-oriented macho guys, and they didn't get along very well. So I didn't have a lot of people coming to my house because my dad was kind of antisocial. I had tons of cousins, but I didn't see most of them. And, my dad didn't like my mom's side of the family at all. He thought they were partiers. They were just happy people. If you hang out with them you see they are fine folks, but since they found my dad to be uptight, they didn't come to visit. I didn't have a lot of friends come to visit because my dad was this gruff, intimidating person. I'm an only child, so I basically grew up spending a lot of time on my own. My mom was kind of isolated as well, especially because my dad didn't want her to have a driver's license. But when we went to weddings or funerals we saw these people who hardly ever came to visit.

The World I Came From

Martina Giselle Ramirez, August 3, 2016

I did not have a history of family success, of uncles and aunts who were lawyers and doctors. I'm an adopted kid who grew up in Pomona, where people in my eighth grade class were incarcerated, and some of them had children out of wedlock. That is the world I came from, but there were people in high school who didn't hold that against me—who could see that I was pretty motivated—and they encouraged me. However, along the way, I also had people just wrote me off because, "Oh, you're brown, you're poor."

Our elementary school had a scholarship program, and I got one of the scholarships that paid part of my tuition while my parents paid the rest. I attended public school in the Pomona Unified School District for three years, and then I started going to Sacred Heart Elementary School. I went there all the way through eighth grade. I graduated in 1973, and then I started high school at this private Catholic high school for boys called Damien High. I went there because my parents were concerned about the public high schools in Pomona. If you wanted drugs, if you wanted gang activity, you just had to go down to a high school in Pomona and you'd find it all.

It was clear that this private high school had a lot more going for it. It was pretty well known nationally because of its debate team. It is in La Verne, which is close to the foothills. On that campus there were a lot of kids from Glendora, Claremont, Upland, and all the other rich foothill communities. If you were coming from somewhere else and you were brown or black, you weren't treated the best way by other students. They sometimes called us "beaners." They would ask what we were doing there, and things like that.

Sacred Heart School had a little scholarship to help students pay for attending Damien High. It wasn't much, but I got it. Because my dad worked hard and my parents were frugal, they could pay the difference in tuition. Thankfully, this was long ago, and the tuition was affordable.

The school was run by an order of priests who treated everybody the same. It was a really great, exceptional experience to be treated so well by the priests. But clearly, there were students there who didn't like us around. I had cousins who had gone there, and those cousins had played football, so basically if you were somebody of color at that school it was assumed that you were on the football or basketball team. Instead, I was in competitive public speaking for four years, I was in student government for three years, and I wrote for the newspaper for four years. I still have four yearbooks from that school.

Some of the other minority children in my eighth-grade class who went to Damien High didn't stay because they got fed up with the lack of acceptance among students, but I was very stubborn. I wasn't going to be taken down by negative comments. I wasn't going to become a statistic. I thought: "If you're going to give me grief about being brown and poor—well let's just see who prevails in the end." And at the end of four years, I became valedictorian. I sought this goal not because I was on an ego trip, but because I thought there needed to be somebody who wasn't a white boy from the foothill communities walking across that stage to give the valedictory speech.

Christine Jorgensen's Book in My School Backpack and Other Childhood Memories

Martina Giselle Ramirez and Alicia Partnoy
August 3, 2016

Martina as a senior at Damien High School, La Verne, California, spring 1977

A: Tell me about your encounter as a kid with Christine Jorgensen's book [*Christine Jorgensen: A Personal Autobiography*]. Do you remember anything about finding the memoir of this transgender pioneer who became internationally known after her gender confirming surgery back in 1952?

M: I went to the Pomona Public Library at least once a week because there was a five-cent book sale when you walked in. I was always reading something and I found very interesting books in that huge library. I remember that there was more written about Jorgensen than just that book. There were articles in the media, so somehow I became aware of her and then I found the book.

A: You just said "somehow." You don't remember any specifics?

M: I just remember being in class reading about her and realizing, "Oh this is like me!" I knew I was different from other people, but I didn't know what that meant, so I often wondered what I was supposed to do.

A: How old were you then?

M: Seventh or eighth grade. So I was probably twelve.

A: And you were looking at this book in class? You took it to class with you?

M: I always had a stash of books in my bag. I was really

efficient at getting assignments done, so I often had time to just do other things.

A: So you weren't worried about reading this book in class. Did you show it to anyone else?

M: When I took it home I didn't show it to anybody there. I had it in my room.

A: And nobody found it?

M: Well, keep in mind I had black widows under my bed [*laughs*].

A: [*laughs*] Really?

M: Yes, my mom didn't know about that.

A: Did you keep them in boxes or—

M: They were in little containers.

A: Oh, so you had this crazy room with spiders since—

M: Since second grade. They were just pets. I never knew that I was going to study spiders as an adult job.

A: Where did you find those spiders?

M: Just around. I was one of those nature-oriented kids. [*laughs*]

A: What were the names of those pets? Do you remember? [*laughs*]

M: No, I don't remember because I always had critters. I had caterpillars, spiders, and a little aquarium that had freshwater pond animals. In a house that I lived in at one point, my room had a long, north-facing window with a six- or seven-foot long shelf. It never got direct sunlight so if you had aquariums there with pond plants and animals, they would do really well. That whole shelf was filled with jars of spiders, insects, and things like that.

A: In your own room?

M: Oh yes, in my own room, which wasn't big. It was a really run-down house. The house is still there, I've driven by and seen it.

A: Did you take pictures of it?

M: I'd have to look because I have thousands of color slides and I started taking pictures at age twelve. By then I wasn't living in that house anymore. We had moved on to a house owned by the same landlord that was a little bigger and better. The first house was kind of falling down. It had a sagging ceiling, and I slept near a water heater, and at night when the water heater would kick on, you could see the flames in there. [*laughs*]

A: Good for your dreams! [*laughs*]

M: I guess! There's hell right there, you better behave [*laughs*]. That house had a lot of issues. In the poor part of Pomona, you took what you could get. At night, I could see from my bed the sagging ceiling. My mom and dad had a room. My little room was in the back, the kitchen was in between, there was a tiny living room, and that was pretty much it. But it had a pretty big yard where my mom grew flowers. There was a big tree in the front yard, a Chinese elm. Chinese elms attract mourning cloak butterflies, so every year there'd be hundreds of caterpillars in that tree. And then they would climb down the tree and up the wall of the house and make cocoons under the eaves. I'd just scoop the caterpillars up and keep them in my room because I could get leaves off the tree to feed them.

Outside with My Camera

Martina Giselle Ramirez, August 5, 2016

Martina emerging from Empire Cave, Santa Cruz, California, May 2018

Taking pictures has been a big part of my life. Around the same time I discovered those books and articles in the library about transgender pioneer Christine Jorgensen, I also got my first camera. We lived across the street from a public golf course. It was long and linear, and there was a big fence with holes in it, so, it was pretty common for the golf balls to come across the street. If you were a local kid in the neighborhood, you collected the balls and when you took them to the golfers they would give you five or ten cents.

Above the golf course there was a big elevated area with homes. I would bike all over the place—it was always me and my bike. I had built my bike out of parts because if you were poor that was what you did, and my dad had all kinds of tools.

The nice thing was that if you biked on that road above the golf course and went around the corner, then you were into old streets. Across the 71 Freeway were some hills that are all covered by homes and developments today, but when I was growing up, it was just open space. Whenever I had a chance, I used to go across the freeway into those hills and wander around. I would see birds and snakes, and much more. There was actually a cave up there at some point but because of safety concerns, it was sealed up.

I used to go up there with my camera. The goal was to get out of my house because my dad was not always pleasant to be around. With neither siblings nor friends coming over very often, that was one of the things I did to get out of the house. I wish I had kept a journal when I was growing up and had written down my reflections while I was wandering around in those hills. I know I pondered how to get out of my situation of poverty, family isolation, and my gender dilemma. I felt my life was so unfair!. At the same time, I couldn't help but admire the beauty of nature, with its trees, flowers, spiders, and other creatures.

I have kept my photos from back then. There are pictures of the backyard when my mom had plants. My mom also used to keep everything, even the articles I wrote as a teenager for the school newspapers, and the little snippets about me in the local papers from when I won awards. I was a competitive public speaker and would get awards from tournaments, so they often were reported in the papers. She saved all those things.

Later on, photography was useful again in graduate school because I needed to take pictures of my research in case I wanted to use them in talks. I was going out in the wild to collect spiders, and wherever I went for my spider research, my camera went. We went to really beautiful places.

For many years, my life was driven by my need to be successful. I felt that I had to do my job as a faculty member really well because I had no financial alternative, and I had a family to support. My life was driven by the feeling that I had to make things work wherever I went. Because my jobs in the 1990s were just for two- or three-year contracts—except for the last one, which was tenure-tracked—I always needed to apply for tons of jobs. I knew I was going back on the job market again in two or three years. I used to tell myself, "You better be productive all the time." So there wasn't much time left for photography.

I have much more space now to be who I am, and I think about a lot of things that for years I just put away because they were too painful. But now, my life is fuller than ever. And for fun, what I like to do on weekends is what I used to do as a kid: go outside with my camera.

Born with XY Chromosomes

Martina Giselle Ramirez, August 3, 2016

A couple of years after I found Christine Jorgensen's autobiography, in which she discusses her experience transitioning from a man to a woman, I became involved in competitive public speaking. I did debate just for a little bit, and I spent a while doing something that is known as "extemporaneous speaking." When you compete in "extemp," as it is known, they give you a subject based on current events, and you have from five to ten minutes to come up with a speech on that subject. People that do it have to be really plugged in to current events.

To be prepared, I would read the *Los Angeles Times* every day, and save articles. I had extensive folders where I collected newspaper articles. During that time, President Nixon was in the process of being impeached. Day by day his administration was collapsing, and then he resigned. This was between 1973 and 1974. Somewhere along the way, I found an article in the *LA Times* about how in the

1960s, a drug called DES (diethylstilbestrol) was given to women during pregnancy to prevent miscarriages. The article described boys who were born to mothers who had taken this drug, and how they found that years later, they were developing breasts.

The point of the article was that researchers had not realized until much too late that the drug had this side effect. Once they did, they immediately outlawed it so that no one could use it anymore. But when I read that article, I actually saved it because it made me get very emotional. I was envious of those boys. Here were people born with XY chromosomes who ended up feminized. They were so lucky! In my mind, if you had to be stuck with this "XY situation," being able to take a drug to develop breasts seemed encouraging. I was fourteen at the time, and that article played a role in my self-discovery. Those were the kinds of articles that I used to hide.

The problem was that though Jorgensen's book and those articles gave me insight into who I was, they also made me extremely sad because I was in this situation where I didn't have money do the kind of things that I had read about concerning gender transition. Even if there was money, my parents were conservative, Catholic, Republican. Even if they had been more open, they still had no money. Moreover, in my parents' world, if you were born with XY chromosomes, you had to be the typical male who did not show emotions. I became extremely good at suppressing my thoughts about being transgender because it was too hard to reflect on such things.

The 70s: On Keeping Up with the News

Martina Giselle Ramirez and Alicia Partnoy,
August 5, 2016

A: Finding Christine Jorgensen's book [about her transition from male to female] in your childhood made you realize that you were not alone, but it also had a negative effect on you, right?

M: Yes, that's right, I lost hope. I knew I could never get this [gender-confirming surgery] for myself. I mean, did we even have health insurance most of my years growing up? No!

A: I'm even surprised that your insurance is paying for your surgery now.

M: Thanks to the Affordable Care Act, or Obamacare. My impression is that when gender-confirming surgeries started making their way into the world, many insurance companies had to add coverage for these kinds of things thanks to the ACA. I don't know the details. But back when I was a kid, I just had to put those thoughts away because otherwise I would get too sad.

A: Did you ever have a speaking contest where this issue came out as something you had to debate?

M: No, the topics were usually not political.

A: But this is not political. [*laughs*]

M: No, but as I said, because I read the whole *LA Times* every single day, I would be like, "What's this? Really? Oh my God." Then I would take it to my room.

A: You kept clippings of the news?

M: Yes, I had file folders full of articles about Nixon's impeachment, the Vietnam war—things that were going on in the 70s. Because you never knew when you were going to get thrown a question about income inequality or civil rights.

Bring Me Your Unloved People and I Will Get Them through the System

Martina Giselle Ramirez, August 5, 2016

In Pomona, California, it was sometimes more than one hundred degrees Fahrenheit in the summer, whereas in Los Angeles it was only around seventy degrees. So when my high school mentor, Barbara Busse, suggested that I apply to Loyola Marymount University, I thought that it was a great idea. Just imagine how exciting it was to think of attending a good school two miles from the beach, where the air was fresh and cool. "This is where I want to go to school," I thought. And that was that.

My first year was intense. In my sophomore year, I worked for the school paper, the *Loyolan*, and I volunteered for Special Games, a kind of mini Olympics for mentally and physically challenged people we held at our school. I was also a founding member of a club, Chicanos for Creative Medicine. I was the one who typed up their constitution.

Then I met a couple of inspiring faculty members who got me thinking about becoming a college professor:

Howard Towner and Floyd Jenkins. Howard taught at LMU for more than thirty years, until he passed away in 2000. He was my academic advisor during my years there, and because we stayed in touch throughout graduate school, he was the one who told me about the job opening for my current LMU faculty position. Howard was a great scientist, but he wasn't one of those ego-oriented PhDs who are full of themselves.

Floyd was the last Jesuit biologist our university ever had. He was a paleontologist and studied fossilized mammals. He would go to Africa in the summer, and he would come back with boxes of dirt from what used to be ancient riverbanks. He hired me as a work-study student, so I usually went to his lab on Friday afternoons. It was my job to sit there for a couple of hours with dental tools looking for these little tiny teeth because the mammals he studied were really small.

Floyd was a funny character. He would sneak up on people and scare them. But he was an amazing teacher. He was the one who told me about the relationship between faith and science. He taught me about a Jesuit paleontologist, Pierre Teilhard de Chardin, who became known worldwide because he tried to show that the world of science and the world of faith were the same reality, just viewed from different perspectives. He studied early human remains, and at some point his ideas were thought to be too cutting edge, so he was not given a lot of love by the Catholic Church. It's fascinating that now there is a Jesuit pope, de Chardin has had a comeback, and the church is giving him some love.

When I came back to teach this time at LMU, Floyd had retired, and he was living in the Jesuit community house on campus. As his health started to decline, I got involved in helping him sort out his belongings. The cool thing is that now, in my Spider Lab, I have his rock hammers and the dental tools that I used when I worked for him as an undergraduate. When Floyd passed away, it was pretty emotional for me. I spoke at his memorial service in Sacred Heart Chapel, and I felt like the baton was being passed from one generation to the next.

During my years studying at LMU, the Seaver College of Science and Engineering faculty was largely male and Caucasian. As a student, I had seen that, especially in my freshman biology class, some of the students of color who were there at the beginning weren't there at graduation. They didn't usually leave LMU, but they changed to other majors. Part of the reason is that class after class, they would seldom see anybody like them in professor roles or in high positions.

Learning about this made me want to change the way this world of academia looked, not just in terms of ethnicity and gender, but also in regard to class. In doing so, I hope to set an example for success. For instance, in the past few months, I have been meeting with Sarah, a student who is transitioning from male to female. We've talked about details big and small as she considers how to navigate her path to transition, socially, medically, and so forth. My life continues to be devoted to helping those students who, because of the color of their skin, because they are poor, because they are gay, lesbian, bisexual, or transgender, have not received support to achieve their dreams. So my idea is, and it might sound more grandiose than it is: bring me your oppressed, your unloved people, and I will get them through the system!

In Survival Mode

Martina Giselle Ramirez, August 5, 2016

When I started dating Rose, whom I later married, the fact that she was a psychology major helped me address some of the emotions I had repressed for a long time. Thinking about how wonderful it was that people could transition, but believing I could never have that myself had been hurting me.

I also grappled with what had been done to my dad because he was not white, so I was always in survival mode. There was no way I was going to go through what he did. And I was pretty set on helping those who were unloved. These reasons gave me strength and helped me be resilient, so I was able to stand up to people. But I was not doing it because I was ego oriented. I was doing it to help the people who were coming behind me. The fact that I had that motivation in my life allowed me not to be reduced to depression by my gender identity dilemma.

Wearing Women's Clothes

. . . .

Martina Giselle Ramirez and Alicia Partnoy
July 25, 2017

A: All the trans narratives I've been reading include references to feelings that arose when the authors presented as women or wore women's clothing for the first time. Can you recall the first time you wore women's clothing?

M: I remember wearing my mom's shoes around the house when my parents weren't around, but it was rare when I was left alone in the house. Did I ever wear any of her clothes? I don't think so. I don't think I had a chance to do it.

A: How could you get those shoes?

M: We had such a small house! Sometimes my mom would go and talk to neighbors and my dad would be out working. The thing about shoes is you get them on and off really fast!

As opposed to getting into a dress or putting it over your head. Because I knew my mom would walk in at any minute.

A: What did you like, high heels?

M: No, because she wasn't into heels. I do know at some point I tried some of her heels, and it was like, "Wait, there are balance issues!"

A: How old were you?

M: I was in elementary school.

A: I was just visiting my friend, and her son, who's nine, walked into the room with her high heels on. We just said, "Ok, good!"

M: It's a different world today.

A: We also told him, "Enjoy them. Don't destroy them!" And you—do you remember the shape, the color of those shoes, or just the fear of being caught?

M: Absolutely not, just the fear. When I did things like that, my heart was beating really fast. Because my mom didn't work outside the house, she was never anywhere else, and when she went somewhere else she had to take me.

A: What about wearing dresses and other women's clothing?

M: The first time that I had a chance to do that was in graduate school when I lived on my own. I had been married to Rose for five years and then we divorced. Somewhere near the end of that year I lived by myself off campus in an apartment in the Santa Cruz mountains. About a year later, we started dating again, and we remarried, but for that year it was just me in that apartment. That was really the first chance that I had to go get stuff, go to Goodwill, go to Target.

A: What did you get?

M: This was the 1980s. I had aerobic wear, because I was a very active person. I had leggings, I had over-sized tops. I remember I had some Reebok high tops from Costco. I was kind of an athletic girl. I was comfortable like that. I was never really into girly kinds of things. For me it was always a sporty girl look. Of course in the Santa Cruz mountains, winter is really cold. I probably had some dresses. I have to think back, but I believe I had mostly skirts and tops. I really didn't have time to go anywhere. I would go to campus a couple of days a week, but most of my time I was in my apartment. I had this dissertation to do, so I spent a lot of time at the computer, doing tons of statistics. Whole days would go by with me running statistical tests and working on my text on the computer, so I could wear whatever I wanted.

A: Then, you were presenting as a woman that year.

M: Pretty much, but not every day, because I had to go to campus sometimes.

A: You did not present as woman on the college campus?

M: No. Because the biologists were kind of close-minded, and I had to worry about my professional life, and of course they were going to have to write letters for me, for jobs. I thought I'd better not do it there. When I started working with students in support programs for underrepresented students, I sometimes presented as female. Not always, but enough to know my way around doing that. By the time I met people like my former student and friend Selene [Perez], it had already been, like, two or three years of dressing *en femme* whenever I could. When I remarried my spouse, I moved back on campus, so I had to go back to presenting as male. Since I was living in the student residences on campus at UC Santa Cruz, I thought it was risky to continue dressing as a woman. When I started working at these jobs after my PhD, for seven years I was presenting as female at work because I figured they were two- or three-year contracts in places where I didn't really want to be for a long time.

A: Do you remember the first time you wore makeup?

M: Selene helped me the first time.

A: Athena [Ganchorre] remembers also going to buy makeup with you.

M: We went shopping. I'd have to think who did it first. Various people went with me on shopping trips, and my friend Athena, another former student, was one of them. Deena Smith, who's in Washington, DC—she was another one. I had this circle of women students who knew about my situation and were like, "Okay, this is cool. We're going to help you." That was so sweet! It was in those seven years in the 1990s when I was presenting as female at work that I got really good. I had a pretty extensive wardrobe. The downside was that I had to change in the car to go to work and had to change again before I went home. That's how it was. I do have pictures of me presenting as female. I remember that there was a conference on evolution in Boulder, Colorado. One of my students, April Boulton, knew about my situation and she would go shopping with me. I have some pictures from that conference. That summer we were also working in the lab together, so there are pictures of us in swimsuits on campus. There's another picture of us collecting spiders in sand dunes in Colorado, and we're both in two-piece swimsuits collecting spiders in the sand.

That was the trajectory, but when I came to Loyola Marymount for my tenure-track job, it was like, "Oh, this is all going to go in the closet and you can't do it anymore!"

This Book and the Elephant Analogy

Martina Giselle Ramirez, August 3, 2016

If you put ten people who have never seen an elephant in a room with an elephant, blindfold them, and then ask them to report what they encounter in that room, each may give a different answer. Somebody might wander around and pull the tail, for example, and that person would think, "Oh, an elephant is in essence a thin, wiggling being." Somebody else might wander up to the front, grab the tusk, and say, "Oh, it's really slick, an elephant is like a shiny car bumper." Then, a third person might grab the ears and think, "Oh, an elephant is like a rug that's hung at a rug store." It's the same animal, yet different people had different slices of the reality in front of them, and only collectively can they get a sense of what an elephant is. This idea is based on an old Indian parable.

To tell my story, we have chosen to include the perspectives of people who can speak about me based on their different experiences and interactions. One person may have known me in one context and point in time, and their perspective would be different from another's, like in the story of the elephant. I see only out of my own eyes, but other people around me can hear chatter like, "Oh wow, what is Martina doing wearing these clothes?" I'm never in those conversations, and there is no video recording of my journey.

I do not see this book as a party of one, where we've got all these balloons and streamers, and it's just me in the room saying, "No one else can come in, I want the cake for myself." Why put a party together without having some folks around? I guess because I was an only child, I value people a great deal. I am so different from my father. He had some opinions that were not going to be swayed, and he tried to get in your face and tell you how you should live. I, instead, look at people as these unique wonders and always ponder how lucky I am to know them. I also value what they say because they see the world through different perspectives and lenses.

I think in terms of photography as well. The photographs that you take capture a particular place in a particular time. You can bring another photographer through the same zoo or park, and they are going to have a different set of images to capture different aspects of the wonder out there. If they both put on exhibits, one will not be better than the other, they will just present two different flavors of reality.

Being Myself in Small Towns

Martina Giselle Ramirez and Alicia Partnoy
August 5, 2016

Martina sunning out with her Master of Science student April Boulton at Bucknell
University, Lewisburg, Pennsylvania, during a long break in lab work, June 1996

A: Was your wife supportive of you presenting as a
   woman?

M: Back in those days, I didn't do it at home. I would take
   a set of clothes in my car, change, and go to work.

A: So she wouldn't find out?

M: No, she knew I was doing that. And I was okay with
   changing because while we were living in these little

towns that were conservative, I didn't want to make it an issue for my girls. So it was an okay compromise. More generally, I think she would've been very happy if I didn't present at all, if my presenting as female just went away.

A: When the kids were little . . .

M: Again, that was not Los Angeles. Those were small towns with a few thousand people. I didn't have a problem with that, but what really wore down our relationship were the years after we moved back to Los Angeles and I started the tenure track job at Loyola Marymount.

A: The years you were not presenting as a woman—when you were not being yourself.

M: That was the kind of situation I was living in when I first got to know you, back in those days.

A: You were super sad, or stressed, or a serious professor. But with the students you were always an approachable mentor, right?

M: Yes. That was a constant, and it was really a lifesaving thing for me. Because that's been the biggest purpose of my life—to help others in this world of science. See, when I grew up, more than once I found people not being supportive and writing me off because I was brown or poor. I'd sit in church and learn about how Jesus treated people. He didn't write off people who had been sleeping with other men, or tax collectors, or people who weren't part of the Jewish faith. So I could see in my world growing up that among people I knew, including my dad, there was a disjunction between what they seemed to believe when we were in church every Sunday, and what they did, how they lived their lives in the real world. For me, it was clear that if I was going to say I believed, then I needed to act accordingly. I became dedicated to people who society didn't think were worth much. I really just didn't want to see other people deal with what I'd had to deal with.

My World Was Declining

Martina Giselle Ramirez, August 3, 2016

The people in my life who have been important romantically are humble and have big hearts.

What drew me to Rose was that she was that way. She grew up a poor person, and she was valedictorian of her high school class, like me. Her grandparents had come over from Mexico in the 1920s or so and they worked on the farms. Her parents moved into the same house where her dad's parents had lived, and that's where she grew up. Her house was quite dilapidated when I started dating her, so I didn't see where she lived until months later. She thought it was embarrassing because it had an outhouse and a sagging ceiling. I could see that she had her own trajectory of coming from poverty to this affluent university, and like me, she had people who encouraged her. I graduated from college in May of 1981, and we got married a month later. She had received a National Science Foundation fellowship, as I had, to go to graduate school and pursue a PhD.

I've seen that people who live through hard upbringings quite often become resilient, and it makes them interested in giving back. However, sometimes when they do become successful, they tell the world, "Look how wonderful I am. I'm the awesome Latino professor. I'm a star." There are indeed people who go down that path of ego. Rose was never that way. She learned about the Catholic Worker Movement when she was at Loyola Marymount University, and she went as a volunteer to Skid Row—the major homeless area in downtown Los Angeles—because of Campus Ministry. I did some of that, but she did more of that work. She was the one who told me about Dorothy Day, the founder of the Catholic Worker movement.

Rose met Jeff Dietrich, one of the founders of the Catholic Workers in Los Angeles. Jeff had a book written about him and was this pioneer of Catholic social justice. So there she was, hanging out with people like that as an undergraduate student, and I admired her. We were on similar life paths; she wanted to go into the world and help people who were underserved, as I did. That nourished our romantic relationship. And that quality has drawn me to all the people in whom I have been romantically interested. I don't really care what they look like, how much money their family has, or if they have a nice car. Unless they have a good soul and a good heart, I'm not interested.

Rose did three years of graduate school in the Biology PhD program. She got out of that after three years and went into the History of Consciousness PhD program. Donna Haraway was her PhD advisor, and she was hanging out with elite luminaries in the world of the history of science in Santa Cruz.

However, after three years, she left that world and

started working as a grant administrator. She ran federally funded minority support programs at Santa Cruz for five years, working with students of color who were supported by the grant that she had obtained for the school. She advised and encouraged them. She was just carrying out her dream of helping people in different ways, rather than by pursuing her PhD.

During the 1990s, when I was getting these two- or three-year jobs, she was being uprooted each time and had to figure out what she could do. When we went to the Claremont Colleges, she got a job at the Upward Bound program in a college helping K–12 public schools with underserved students. She did that for two years and had a great time. At those schools there were many kids with parents similar to our own parents, students who were not expected to achieve because they were brown and poor. This federally funded program was sprinkling money to help them make it, and that was another way Rose's vision played out. Later, when we went to Bucknell University, she went to work for a crisis hotline for three counties. Rose would ride with police officers who took people to mental institutions or hospitals. Again, she was helping people in need.

However, I knew that there were going to be challenges with the way our lives were evolving. Our move to Los Angeles basically left me as the only person earning money and supporting the household for all those years. I didn't have a problem with her not making money for a couple of years, but at some point it was like my whole life revolved around work, doing summer school and extra work during the school year. Inside I was crying, "Can't you see that my world is declining?"

I had no friends my age because my whole life was driven by work. That was when things started becoming problematic. I thought that I had married someone who was going to be there for me, but I felt our relationship becoming more and more unbalanced.

I also wondered if Rose realized how hard it was for me to go from being open about who I was during the 1990s to having to hide again for so many years in Los Angeles. It was not easy for me to do that.

Interview with Selene Perez—Part 1: Martina Was Unhappy as Martin

Martina Giselle Ramirez and Alicia Partnoy
August 23, 2017

Selene Perez and Martina, July 2017

A: Selene, can you tell me a bit about yourself and your career?

S: I work in biotech. My undergraduate degree was in marine biology. A friend got me into biotech, and I've been doing it ever since I finished college. I grew up in Southern California. I'm of mixed heritage. My father is second-generation Mexican-American—his mother came over from Mexico when she was five—and my mother is Caucasian. Her people are from Arkansas and have been [in America] since before the Civil War—they were actually there during the Civil War. So, a very mixed background.

A: Where did you meet Martina?

S: I met her back in 1990 during my freshman year of college at UC Santa Cruz. I was with my parents in an orientation session, I think it was through the Academic Community of Excellence. Maybe a meet and greet. And I could be wrong, but it was some sort of social event, and she was there with her wife and daughter, who was around two years old. My parents and I met her there. Well, back then she was Martin.

A: And what was your first impression of her?

S: She was very personable, and my parents liked her too. Very knowledgeable and personable. I think the easiest way to say it is that she made an impression on everybody because of her intelligence and just the way she had about her.

A: Had you declared your major?

S: I always knew I was going to be a biology major. I just ended up taking a lot of classes around marine biology. Mainly because I felt more at peace and was more interested in being in the outdoors versus being in the lab. I felt more comfortable with the professors that did work outside the lab. The easiest way to say it is that the ones who work outside the lab have more developed social skills.

A: Selene, did you continue seeing her when she was Martin on campus? How did your connection grow?

S: She told me about herself, about identifying as a woman, I think in the first quarter of my freshman year. She had an office at home. I think I went over to her house. They [Martin and Rose] lived on campus at the time. And I went there, I can't remember exactly why, but it had something to do with classes. When she told me about everything, obviously I was a little bit shocked because I didn't know about transgender people. When I grew up, it was not something that was talked about.

A: Right. That's true.

S: So it took me a bit, I was a little shell shocked I guess, or just processing. It's not like I didn't talk to her, I asked her questions and she was very frank and open about her answers. I think some of the questions I asked her were about the fact that she was married, with a child, and how her partner felt about this. One thing that I couldn't grasp at the time was that she was with a partner who, according to my perception of the situation, wanted to ignore that aspect of her. And then I was like, "Okay, well if you feel this way, why are you still acting like a man?" I didn't understand that part even after she explained to me her reasons, which were valid. Here she is in the field of sciences at a university . . . the easiest way of saying it is that universities are very conservative, even if they are not religious. She said it would "be harder for me in my line of work to get a job and move up to get tenure if I'm living the way I feel." My answer was, "Ok, fine, but we only have one life to live."

A: You said that back then? You told her that? Wow!

S: Yeah! This is an ongoing argument or discussion we have had since then. I never understood two things. Number one, why she was with someone who didn't totally accept her for who she was. And number two, was she going to tell her child these things? Because my understanding was that this was something she did in the closet—something no one knew about—a dirty little secret. Well, eventually her child was going to find out, and the discussion we had over the years was the same. After they had their second daughter, I kept telling her that the girls were going to find out. I said, "The issue I have around this is that they're going to be shocked. It's one thing if you do it as they're growing up, as 'This is just an aspect of dad. This is who he is, this is just an aspect and we accept him as he is.' If you put this in the closet, and they find out about it later, they will feel they grew up living a lie." And [they'd feel like] they didn't even know this person, their father. The girls would be traumatized when this eventually came out. How long could she live like this and actually be happy? That was the discussion we had for years. Meanwhile, she moved back East and then came back to California. I saw her again when she was in Pomona, I think about sixteen years ago, and I could tell she wasn't happy.

And I would tell her again, "Look, you've been living like this for so many years. You're not happy. There's a community down there. Why don't you hook up with the community, and at least you will be able to go somewhere where you feel like you can be yourself and learn?" Because one thing that I realized from interacting with her was that I didn't know how many unspoken societal norms you learn as a girl growing up, things she had not been taught.

A: Yeah, [*laughs*] I realize that.

S: When I was still in Santa Cruz, she would put these outfits together. I was like, "Girl, what are you doing?" You absorb all these things about how society expects you to behave as a woman or a girl. How you dress, how you do your makeup. You take it for granted, and here she's got to learn it. She didn't have that community.

A: You were very mature as a young student. Do you know if other students were, like you, having deep discussions with her?

S: I don't know, I can't remember if I ever mentioned it to anybody else. I probably mentioned it to my parents, and later on, when I found out she transitioned a couple of years ago, I told them. I had lost contact with Martina for a number of years, mainly on my part because I couldn't stand seeing her so unhappy. That's why I stopped talking to her. I don't think I told her that, but I couldn't stand seeing her like that.

A: You were suffering.

S: Yeah, it was hard to see her so unhappy. And I was like, "You need to change."

A: You know, when I met her as a professor, as Martin, here on campus, that was my impression. What happened with this person? Why is he so serious, so upset? He seemed to be upset with us when we were together with the Latino faculty. I think he was feeling very uptight, constrained in that environment. With some of the former students I spoke to, I don't think they caught the unhappiness the way you describe it. Now, she is like a totally different person for me. That's why the title of the book is *Happier as a Woman*. But then, other former students, they never described this unhappiness that I did perceive and that you talk about. It was not so obvious for other people.

S: The other thing is that I put myself in her shoes: How would I feel if I had to live the way that she described? I would be very unhappy, because you're constantly living a lie. You are living for someone else's expectations. You're not living your life for you.

The Things I Do Today, I Learned from My Mother

Martina Giselle Ramirez and Alicia Partnoy
August 3, 2017

Helen Ramirez and Martina Giselle Ramirez, July 2016

M: You want to know more about my mom?

A: Yeah, because I was very moved by the picture that you took with her at the nursing home. You said that she was your first model of a woman. And now, judging from her reaction to your transition, I think that, even if she can't say it with words, she is a model in terms of open-mindedness too.

M: We can't have a conversation. She can't speak or write since her stroke.

A: But I can see her enjoying your visit, the first time she sees you presenting as woman. She suffered abuse in her relationship. Do you think she is a model of a resilient woman?

M: Yes, because she had to make the best of a bad situation for years and years. My dad was hard to get along with, and besides, we didn't have much money. She got really good at mending things and making yummy food with the little that we had. I admired her a lot because she put up with my dad for so long. She was a happy person, but it was really hard for her. In fact, her whole side of the family were these happy people, and then there were all those Ramirez brothers who were kind of stuck up and had issues, and never smiled.

My love of going to yard sales and secondhand stores, my ability to fix things—I got those from her. I saw her doing that because she had no other choice. Many other things that I do today I learned from her, like the fact that I have plants near my doorstep and that my dining table is covered with plants. She always had a garden, and it was part of my job to go out and weed it. What better way to have breakfast than to have these things of beauty on your table while you eat? She was really good at getting things to grow, and now I'm good at that too. I never had a chance in all those years to think about having my own garden, and now I do, so I'm always looking to acquire this plant or that plant. I think so much of that came from her. We also were very religious. We went to church everyday.

Martina with her home garden, April 2018

A: Every day?

M: Yes, early in the morning.

A: Did you meet a lot of people who went to Mass every day?

M: There were the regulars, ten or fifteen people, and they had the Masses in the little chapel. And I was an altar server.

A: You had that job every day?

M: Not all the time. There was a schedule. When I was in high school I was a lot busier than in elementary school and could not go so often. But once I could drive, I usually drove my mom during the summers.

A: Every single day, before going to elementary school, the three of you would go to church where you listened to reflections about how to be a better human being?

M: Yes, usually, but my dad worked in real estate at some point so his schedule was his own.

A: I don't think I ever met someone who went to church every day as a child.

M: Keep in mind, this is a family that also read the Bible from start to finish together. And then, we would go back to the beginning and read it again. It took months to do these kinds of things. When I was in high school, life was different, I don't remember doing that. But their Catholic faith was big in their lives. Because I was such a thoughtful person, I found the beatitudes so beautiful: love is patient, love is kind, love knows no barriers.

A: And your mom was like that?

M: In her own way. Those things for me matter a lot, so when people are boastful or full of themselves, I want to say, "No. Look what it says in the Bible." The business of treating people as worthy of respect makes sense. Just look at what Jesus does. He doesn't insult people or put them off. He hangs out with tax collectors and other hated people. Society says, "Oh she's been with five men, she's sleeping around." But Jesus hangs out with people like her. In the Bible you also see him telling it like it is to people in authority. He criticizes them for what they're doing, and that is awesome.

As a kid, those things mattered to me. People talked about living the examined life, and I don't think I did it to an extreme, but I did it. I just felt that if you're going to say you believe, then you should make sure the way you live life matches that. That plays out in what I do with people who don't get much love or respect—women, underrepresented and first-generation students. The origin of my actions stems from having been mistreated often for who I was, but also because those religious values made sense to me. The examples of Jesus, Buddha, and other religious folks make sense to me.

A: Were the services at church ever in Spanish?

M   Some of them, depending on the day.

A: I'm interested in your relationship with the language.

M: Well, keep in mind that my parents never taught me
    Spanish because when they grew up they were in a
    segregated school system, where you were penal-
    ized for speaking Spanish in class. They knew how
    to speak Spanish just fine, but they never taught me
    Spanish.

A: And they never spoke Spanish at home?

M: Right, so really my learning of Spanish happened
    when I took it for three years in high school. That's
    when I learned it.

A: Maybe I alienated you by speaking Spanish when
    I first met you and you were that serious professor.
    [laughter]

The Letter to My Mom

Martina Giselle Ramirez, December 24, 2014

Dear Mom,

I have been thinking about doing this letter for quite a while, but now that final exams, grading, and other things are done, I have some free time for a change.

First, I want to say how very sorry I am for not coming to visit you in quite a long time. It's not been about busyness really, rather, it's been a matter of being uncertain about whether I should go visit or not.

Which brings me to this letter, which concerns something we never talked about—my nature—and now sadly, the outcome of your stroke makes that impossible. And so, this letter will have to do for now.

First, let me say that if having a conversation about this matter via this letter is something you would rather not have, just let Rose know and she will stop right here. But if you are willing to listen to what are some very personal and heartfelt thoughts, I'd like to share my story as it has unfolded in recent years.

In any case, as I think you know from Rose, I have started on the path toward doing a gender transition, in order to finally live in a way that is true to myself. This is something that has been in my mind since about seventh or eighth grade but given life circumstances and limited finances along the way, I never thought I would be able to substantially act on this during my lifetime. While I did present as female at work for about seven years during the time when I had those temporary faculty jobs back in the 1990s, I was barely making enough money to support the family and health plans at the time did not cover transitions, and so doing more was out of the question.

Coming back to LA in 1999 was a challenge in many ways, financially and otherwise, and since I did not know how being open about my trans nature would go over at LMU, I hid that aspect of myself . . . for eleven long years . . . which was very difficult. Indeed, it seemed so sad that while I always encouraged my students to be "true to themselves" and to "live their dreams," I was not doing that for myself. By 2010, the many years of pretending to be less than I was, along with the hard life I've had here—working seven days a week, month after month, year after year in the endless quest for yet more money, with no friends my age, much less time to find any—was all too much.

While all that work made for a successful career and a stellar reputation campus-wide and beyond, as well as obviously providing the financial basis for the family's well-being, the cost for me personally was very high, especially since I could not even be myself while doing all those tasks with excellence. In any case, trans folk are known to have higher rates of depression and suicidal thoughts, and I could tell I was drifting in that direction. So, I needed to do something positive for myself . . . and so in summer 2010, I began my journey of starting to present as female once again . . . and later, doing more.

What I have learned along the way is how times have changed! Coming out as trans at LMU and beyond has gone quite smoothly, quite a contrast to the sometimes chilly reception I got from some people back in the 1990s. This was never a big deal with LMU students after I came out as trans, and in fact, it has increased my standing in their eyes to be doing so at my age. Along the way, I have gotten all manner of gifts from them, ranging from clothes to makeup to bras to gift cards, with even some moms joining in the "getting her stuff" action. It was the student example that set the tone for the faculty/staff, with pretty much everyone getting on board quickly with the use of the correct gender pronouns, etc. Given this context, it made sense for me to change my name on campus in spring 2013, something that became legal in all contexts when I had a court ordered name change in Feb. 2014. In Aug. 2014, I also got a CA driver license which shows my new name and lists my gender as "F."

The other big development that has helped with this process is that several major health plans now cover this in their policies. That's the reason I switched to Kaiser in Jan. 2014. As part of this process, I'm required to live full time as a woman, this being facilitated by being on hormone therapy, which I started in May 2014. Since it has been over 7 months now, much has changed for me, both physically and otherwise. While I am the same person in terms of values, vision, motivation, humility, kindness, and so forth, that basis has seen additions/enhancements in many ways. And so, here are some highlights of what life is like for me as 2014 comes to a close:

1. Hair grows back more slowly, though does not go away (that's why I have been having electrolysis sessions for hair removal on my face since Aug. 2013).
2. Pores in my skin have become narrower and my skin has become softer & thinner.
3. I go pee more often [testosterone (T) blocker does that], and so know what it's like standing in line waiting for a stall to open.
4. I am less strong when working out at the YMCA compared to guys (the reduced T level means less strength).
5. I feel cold more easily & need to watch my weight more than before (due to lower metabolism).
6. I have boobs now (I got bra sized at a Victoria's Secret store on Labor Day—I'm an A cup).
7. I never know when something I see/experience/become aware of will get me teary (among other things this fall—a movie clip, a book passage, a choir piece).
8. I have a tendency when someone does something annoying to feel hurt more so than getting angry . . . that is, there is less "fire" than in the old days . . . and what is there dissipates fast.
9. I have an enhanced awareness of male-type patterns of leadership/behavior and how some of that is not at all conducive to people's happiness & self-worth, esp. if one is female [I became director of a campus office this year (see the brochure in the binder), and so have

been present much more in the corridors of power @ LMU . . . and have generally not liked what I have seen in terms of examples of leadership . . . which is why I will probably try for a position in that higher realm someday, to show people how to lead in a kind & humble way].

Finally, I have been told by others who have known me for a long time that I seem happier now . . . they point to the images of me they see on Facebook as evidence, among other things. And I know they are right. Guess that comes of being true to oneself. In any case, this letter comes with a photo album of me in 2014, so take a look.

At the same time, I know that what I am doing has brought grief and uncertainty to Rose and the girls . . . and that has not been fun for me either. I am well aware that my place in the girls' futures is now likely to be very different than what they had imagined. I also know that dealing with this change has been especially hard on Rose, as she has been the key player on the home scene and with the girls, given the way the LMU job has consumed my life. While I wish this could all be easier for everyone, all I can do is live my life according to the dictum "to thine own self be true" and go from there. While I will of course continue to support everyone financially, I know that who I've become is a source of embarrassment and/or discomfort . . . which I find sad. For this reason, I have never shared with them all the details I have put into this letter and have assumed a low/disengaged profile on the home front . . . though I hope there is healing in this regard at some point down the line.

Well, there you have it. . . more personal sharing than you have probably ever heard me engage in! That is another outcome of my transition . . . being able to share more easily about things that matter. Rose and the girls don't see that at home, as I have alluded to above, but people at LMU and elsewhere have . . . and now you have as well.

In closing, please pray for me! And if you would like to have me come visit, just tell Rose and I'll arrange to do so.

Merry Christmas,
Martina Giselle Ramirez

Women as Role Models

· ·

Martina Giselle Ramirez and Alicia Partnoy
July 25, 2017

Barbara Busse and Martina Giselle Ramirez, April 2015

A: All trans narratives I have read mention women as role
    models. Janet Mock, for example, chose her name out
    of admiration for Janet Jackson. Her mom was not so
    much of a role model for her, because her own life had
    been destroyed, but she had a friend she admired. Can
    you think of women role models in your childhood or
    in your teenage years?

M: One of them would be my high school public speaking coach, Barbara Busse. I went to an all-boys Catholic high school with not a lot of women faculty. She was the advisor to the newspaper, and I was on the newspaper staff. I was also on the speech and debate team, and she was our coach. I had a strong connection with her. She was impressive because she could easily navigate through this male world, the religious order of priests who ran the school, and the lay faculty, mostly men. I learned how to be a good public speaker from her, how to control my mannerisms. That's why the voice training that I've been doing recently has been so interesting. My voice coach from Kaiser Permanente says it is not just about voice, it's also about the other accessories to conversation as a woman, like expressive hand movements. In public speaking that stuff is considered distracting unless it adds to what you're saying. You must be thoughtful about what you do or don't do. If you're just a woman conversing with your friends, none of this calculating how to move our hands is necessary, you just move them. In terms of women, I had a very small world.

A: Aunts?

M: Because my dad was antisocial, and didn't want to see them, they didn't come to the house.

A: What about other school teachers? There no impressive models?

M: In terms of people that caught my mind, I don't think so.

A: And the women in the books you read? [Transgender pioneer] Christine Jorgensen was a role model, right?

M: Pretty much. My life has been about how you take the things you have been given and mobilize them for the benefit of others. Anybody who has made a deep impression on me would have been someone who acted that way.

A: And Barbara Busse, was she aware of your gender identity?

M: No. Remember, because it was unsafe at home, I repressed things. I put that stuff away and didn't think about it because it was too painful. I knew that I wasn't as people thought I was, but living in that house was in a way like living in prison in terms of my identity. Otherwise, I was a happy kid and I liked doing science, and I spent more time with girls in elementary school. I knew where I'd rather be and with whom I'd rather hang out.

A: You mostly had women friends, then?

M: If I could, but some would not mix, you know how that works.

A: And they can be pretty obnoxious. I only had one female friend in elementary school, because the other girls had these cliques. They could be really cruel.

M: Because I was an only child, I was good at staying on

my own, so I spent recess looking at spiders or staying in the classroom. When I went to the all-boys high school, there were no women my age around.

A: But Barbara, as your teacher, was very supportive, and gave you all the tools [you needed] to blossom.

M: Barbara took people from all different backgrounds, because I wasn't the only one who didn't have much but went to that upper-crusty rich school. She treated everybody the same, and she took an interest in where our talents were, and how to move them forward, to get them better. I got to know her really well. She had a big impact on me because my career has been based partly on the fact that in the world of scientists, not a lot of people can discuss their knowledge in a way that others understand. For me that has been easy, since I perfected my craft under her tutelage when I was a teenager.

My Life Is Not All about the Transition

Martina Giselle Ramirez, July 25, 2017

I could always tell that there were people around me trying to make me go away. But I was not going to allow the system to eliminate me. At the root of my work and my persistence, there was never the need to prove that I was a successful brown person who became a professional and had a nice car. No, I have walked through this world always trying to pay back, and to help those who were coming after me.

For example, since 1992 I have been teaching a course called Minorities and Women in Science. Students in that class learn about the nature of underrepresentation based on ethnicity and gender. Over the many years I've offered that class, most of the students haven't been science majors and most have been women. Although they're learning about these issues in a science context, they learn a set of skills for coping with the challenges associated with being a professional woman, skills that are easily transferrable to what they might be experiencing in the fields of film and television, business, or in any other male dominated profession. Therefore, as I point out to people, I don't think that my life would have been a failure if I never got to transition gender-wise. As you can see, my life is not primarily about that.

Rereading Jorgensen

. . . .

Martina Giselle Ramirez and Alicia Partnoy
August 5, 2016

A: I saw you were posting on Facebook about rereading [transgender pioneer] Christine Jorgensen's autobiography. Is this the same edition you read as a child?

M: No. I have the 2000 version, but I ordered the 1968 paperback through interlibrary loan because I really want to see that Bantam edition.

A: That's the one you read as a child? Why?

M: Because it's a paperback and it's small, which would make sense. I looked online and it says the paperback sold 40,000 copies. There is an older one, a hardback from 1967, but I've never heard of that publisher. So it looks like Bantam got the book very quickly, and published it immediately.

A: Do you recall any of it now while you read it again?

M: Not the text exactly, but I remember having read about the experiences that she discusses. When I saw this back then, I felt like, "Oh, I know what that's like!" It's kind of cool, because I'm only on chapter 1 and I've already read things that sound familiar.

A: It's interesting how the media and reviewers back then presented her as very glamorous. It's sort of the same trend we observe today, when trans people are never seen just as regular people.

M: That's right! They have to be like models, ready for the fashion runway! [*laughs*] Back then, it was kind of the same deal. Media just globs onto this glamour thing. Christine Jorgensen mentions that what she was wearing got a lot of attention, but no questions were generally asked about what she thought or how she felt.

A: But when people read her book, they learn about her as a human being rather than about this soldier-to-bombshell transformation.

M: Indeed! She is reflecting back on the years around 1952, when her story hit the news, but she's writing the book in 1967. She had some years to reflect. She looked at everything published about her—newspapers, periodicals, journals, scandal magazines, et cetera.

A: So Christine researched and wrote this book all by herself?

M: Yes. Susan Striker wrote the prologue, and then Christine wrote on page three, "Never once in all those acres in newsprint had I been asked about my faith and beliefs, both of which had played important roles in my life. What I slept in apparently was considered more important than what I believed in." It gets back to this idea that the media wants to present these perfectly bodied individuals that have had access to all kinds of technology, are wearing the most wonderful clothes on the planet, and are ready for a glamour magazine. But how much can that reflect reality? I'm hoping it's better today. I haven't read what's been written about Caitlyn Jenner or Laverne Cox, for example. When people who don't know anything about this, like the ones I met when I lived in the midwest, hear about a transgender woman, their knee-jerk reaction is to say, "Oh that's just because the person likes pretty clothes." It all boils down to the externals. Hardly ever do people think about what's going on with your feelings, your thoughts.

A: But beliefs and values don't have a gender, right? So many stereotypes to break! I, for instance, don't care at all about pretty dresses, and I hate makeup. Do you like makeup?

M: Well, it depends. Keep in mind that to me, every person is on a spectrum from really masculine to really feminine. I think that's mentioned in Jorgensen's book, and it's really true. Before I started facial hair removal three years ago, I used to put on makeup pretty regularly because I was trying to cover scratches from shaving. That was really the only reason. I exercise in the morning for an hour and a half, and then I try to get to work by nine. I really don't have time to add in another half hour of doing makeup. So I put on makeup when I go to special events, but that's pretty much it. Once there was enough hair removal done on my face, I stopped worrying about it. But there are students who won't leave their apartment on campus until they are put together for the day, while others don't waste any time putting on makeup, and they are all happy people. I know from years and years of seeing women that they are all on a spectrum.

A: You often speak about how people do not realize that before transitioning you were the same human being you are today in term of values. What shocks the world is the external transformation.

M: Right? Jorgensen, for example, writes about an episode while performing at a club and eavesdropping on two women talking after her show. One of them seemed shocked because Christine looked feminine and appeared to be a fashion model. Then she added that some publication had reported that Jorgensen was engaged or married. To her question on whether that could be possible, her friend replied, "Anything is possible, but I wonder what she's really like personally."

A: So, there is that glimpse! The quote was from a woman, but did you read about how men were talking about her?

M: That's something else. "'What is she really like personally?' That question echoed in her mind and led her to go through all the printed material about her. She then realized the degree to which her persona was sensationalized by the press, and she was concerned about it. She mentions that the media had labeled her from male homosexual to woman seeking to earn money and fame by posing as a transgender person, with many other insulting labels in between.

A: I know. It's infuriating. Do you see the media now fixated on the physical gorgeousness of the body, in the case of trans men?

M: Clearly society has an issue—from what I can tell—with people going from masculine to feminine. Trans men seem to be a lot less in the public eye. People have issues with them as well, but for some reason, there's this big bugaboo about those of us who decided to go into the feminine world.

A: Trans men suffer many attacks, but I realized that, at least in Latin America, the killings of trans women is frequent. However, one of the slogans at the demonstrations against feminicide all over Latin America, "We want ourselves alive," is inclusive of trans women. I wonder who speaks up to stop violence against transgender men.

Painting the Sky with Stars

. . . .

Martina Giselle Ramirez, July 29, 2016

For many years before my transition, I would tell my students to live according to their calling in life. I would tell them that they were going to get messages from their parents and from other people, but that at the end of the day, they would have to ask themselves what they thought their purpose in the world was. For example, I'd say, if you're a religious person, ask yourself—how does that play out in your life? Do you think you are a part of God's plan for the world? I advised students to do what they felt was important to them.

Before, I would be advising young women to be authentic, and I would watch them become successful and be true to their dreams, yet I wasn't doing what I was preaching. Today, while I still live my vocation to support those who face many obstacles, I can finally be fully who I am. This makes it easier for me to smile and be happy.

You must keep in mind that, because I have been

taking pictures since I was twelve years old, I tend to think in images. For many things I imagine in life, I try to think how they would look. I have seen the impact that media, movies, and literary works had on me. When I think of analogies, I try to make them easy to understand. For example, everybody goes to Las Vegas—or tries to—if they live in Southern California. While there, they might get to watch an ice sculptor transform masses of ice into all manner of creations, from corporate logos to wedding reception centerpieces. While the sculptor works, slivers of ice accumulate on the floor or fly off as they are shaved away, shiny examples of the beauty of the whole ice mass. If you think of the whole mass as the Divine, those little slivers are unique aspects of the Divine. I see the students as those slivers. This perspective infuses my drive to help students develop a sense of themselves and their gifts, so they will be ready for the Olympics of life.

Another image that I like to use is inspired by a song. If you come to my office, you will see on one of its walls an album cover from Enya, a New Age artist who has been around for a long time. One of her greatest hits CDs from 1997 is called *Paint the Sky with Stars*. The album art features an artist painting stars on a dark sky. For me, that artist represents me, with the stars being the students or people that I help, because they will give light to a world that has darkness and challenges, even after the artist walks away. I tell my students, "Remember, you are one of those stars, you are one of those luminary things out there." I encourage them to keep the love going no matter what they do in life. When I am gone from this earth, I will have left all those luminaries in a dark world.

Being Brown, Getting Static

Martina Giselle Ramirez and Alicia Partnoy
August 5, 2016

A: Do you remember a moment in which you became aware of being brown?

M: Oh, I'll give you an example but there's more than one. When I was an undergraduate student here, at Loyola Marymount University, there was a faculty member, Professor D. I was in his class. At some point, I was in a meeting with him and I got the strange feeling from the conversation that I was being dissuaded from wanting to go to graduate school. When I shared this experience with my parents, they got upset. They could clearly tell his attitude toward me was strange. They found it appalling at our Jesuit school. Here was someone giving me this subtle message that I shouldn't pursue higher education. Why? Because of who I was?

A: What did he say exactly?

M: I don't recall. I just remember sitting in his office and telling myself, "Wait, am I sort of being given some static here?"

A: Where in your career were you?

M: I think it was during my sophomore year. Maybe I was not doing so well in a class. But he was like: "Oh are you really serious about this?" I was sitting there wondering if I would be getting that message had I been someone else.

A: And earlier, as a child, did you experience these feelings?

M: Yes, at Damien High School, a Catholic all-boys school. Most students there came from the rich surrounding communities. I remember that during my freshman year, some of my friends from Pomona and I were walking to the bike racks to get our bikes and go home after school. As we were unlocking our bikes, a car drove by, and some Damien seniors yelled, "What are you beaners doing here?" as they left the parking lot. I was often under the impression that nobody expected positive things to come out of Pomona.

Reading Susan Faludi: Not in the Darkroom

Martina Giselle Ramirez and Alicia Partnoy
August 24, 2016

M: The doctor who's going to do my surgery in December talks about this book I just got by Susan Faludi.

A: *In the Darkroom?*[3] There's a lot of excitement about it.

M: It's really amazing and I think it can help us with our book project. From what I can tell, Faludi goes to a university library that has a great collection of trans narratives. She reads as many of them as she can and then she reacts at the ways people portray themselves. It's pretty impressive.

A: And her writing is engaging too, right?

M: Oh, of course! Her dad is such a weird character! She said that even before his transition, at Faludi's childhood home, he led this life where there was an emotional curtain, and you couldn't get to know him. He had this standoffish attitude. Then he goes away for twenty-five years, comes back and reconnects, but now he's not male anymore, he's female. The father has a totally different persona than she did before, so it's really pretty amazing.

A: And how old was this guy?

M: He was a teenager during the Nazi occupation.

A: Hungary, right?

M: Right. A very complex life. The father had seen family members get killed. He eventually turns into this big-time photo editor for fashion magazines. Darkroom work, magazine covers—that's where the title *In the Darkroom* comes from. Faludi writes that there are parallels with Jorgensen's book, since Christine's focus is also on photography.

A: We have a common thread, because I also think of you and the important role of photography in your life. That's why I checked out [Mariette] Pathy Allen's book, *The Gender Frontier*.[4] Photography is at its core too: the gaze, who's looking at the transgender people, and how the photographer's eye captures their dignity instead of portraying them as weird characters.

M: I haven't gotten far enough into Faludi's book to see why her father got attracted to photography. He eventually does movies, too, so she talks about him walking around with a movie camera when she's growing up and filming the family.

A: From what I have read, it's obviously hard for Faludi to understand her father's actions. There's a lot of resentment for what she had to endure as a child from this aloof father who abandoned the family. And that translates in a portrayal of the trans father as a weird character. At the end of the day, in her book, the readers stand in solidarity with Faludi, not with the father. Our work seeks to build that solidarity around you, and by extension, around all marginalized transgender people.

M: Right! Also, Susan Faludi says that in the narratives she examined, there is a common pattern of people trying to lock the life they had before they transitioned in the closet. Their message is, "That person is dead and gone. I'm never going to go there." It's like they're totally reborn into this new being.

A: Her own father did that. He disappeared from her life.

M: He divorced her mom and at some point, he moved out of the country. He had been in the US with his mom and then moved back to Hungary, where he had lived as a child. I haven't figured out whether her father thought her life prior to transition was dead or locked away. For me, the story that I had before hasn't gone away, it's not something I want to lock away.

A: Society seems to have an easier time dealing with that approach, but it would be alienating for you, right?

M: Because those years of serving others are a big part of my life, I'm not going to turn my back on them. Also, it's so important to put a different story out there into the world. If you're in my situation and all you see is people with money and glamour and fame transitioning, it's hard not to become depressed, or even attempt suicide, because you don't see any road ahead that is not populated by people who have millions of dollars.

Election Week 2016: Mourn, Resist, Organize

Martina Giselle Ramirez, November 11, 2016

Tuesday, election night, was a very long one as Hilary Clinton (DEM) eventually lost to Donald Trump (REP) by a very close margin. I try not to dwell on it. I am dismayed to know that, in the days since the election, there have been incidents on college campuses and K–12 schools with people going around spewing hateful words at Latino-looking students. This morning I posted on Facebook about junior high kids parading around their school screaming, "Build the wall!" I was appalled to see Donald Trump's intention to build a wall between the US and Mexico to stop immigration echoed and naturalized by those young people.

Today, in my freshman seminar course, we had a conversation for the first ten minutes about the elections. One student told me that her friend goes to a women's college. She said that her friend was in her dorm and that a vehicle filled with a bunch of men screaming political slogans went by. At some point, the vehicle stopped in front of an African American dorm, and the truck's occupants started spewing racial slurs at the people there. Because of this election, many people who might have been reluctant to be open about their views now feel emboldened and feel that they don't need to stay in the shadows anymore. That is extremely wrong.

I have always had some hope in the common sense of the public. However, because I read the *LA Times* and *The New York Times* every day, I have access to detailed political analysis. I saw that, while there was a greater number of Latinos and other groups voting, at the end of the day, more disaffected white people voted too. I'm talking about people who feel put-upon because they fear their jobs are going away.

I was really depressed on Wednesday—mourning. Then, by Thursday, I put things in perspective, thinking about the persecuted early Christians, the people operating under oppression in the Soviet Union for decades, the people in Latin America . . . I just thought, "It will be like this for the next four years."

I felt the need to post a link to an article from *The Nation* entitled, "Mourn. Resist. Organize. These Are Our Tasks Now."[5] on Facebook yesterday. I printed out the title and posted it in my office. I reminded myself that I had been in this awful place many times before. People often did not support me. It happened in so many different ways, and in diverse circumstances, but I did not let that stop me. For example, I was plus sized, I was brown, I was poor, I was first-generation American, and obviously transgender. I did not get a lot of love along the way for being one or more of those things.

But I did not let those people who were cruel to me keep me down. I was certainly mindful of what I needed to do to navigate the obstacles they were putting in my way. So I am just going to keep doing what I'm doing for the next four years: providing support for the values in which I believe, and helping other people do the same.

Not a Happy Week

. . . .

Martina Giselle Ramirez and Alicia Partnoy
November 11, 2016

A: You just walked into my office and told me that it was
not a happy week for you. Is there something wrong
in your life, besides the upsetting results in the [presi-
dential] elections this week?[6]

M: No, everything else is fine, but I was in Ohio for five
days, and also my car was stolen a couple of weeks
ago. But then I got it back.

A: Is it in one piece? When people on Facebook were all
stressed out because your car was stolen, what made
you say, "It's no big deal?" You said something about
enjoying public transportation. I didn't know if you'd
had some wine. . . . [*laughter*]

M: No, no I didn't have wine. I said that because my pool
of happiness has gone up so much in a year that even

though they took my car, I knew I'd have another car, and it would be newer, and it wouldn't be rusting. I knew at some point if I just held out, this inconvenience would go away. See, I was able to use this bike! I bought this bike from a student, and it had just been sitting there for two years. After I filed a police report about my stolen car and the police left, I spent the afternoon walking to the store to get a chain and lights for my bike. I cleaned it up because it had been sitting there for two years out in the open. So, I made it really nice and then, later that day, I rode it to campus.

A: How did you feel?

M: Well it was a lot of work climbing that hill. I don't want to do that every day, but at least I know I can do it. I figured this was just a chance for me to experience a different way of getting around the city. And I really loved the ride along the Ballona Creek Channel because the water is next to it. I used to do that five or six years ago, when I couldn't run anymore. There were like two or three weeks when I was riding every day for eight to ten miles a day.

A: But, did you say that you got the car back? The night I went to your neighborhood for the first time, I told my husband that it was such a nice neighborhood and that there were all these expensive new cars there. Why did they steal your very old car?

M: Who knows?

A: Did you ever think it could be a hate crime, and that they could be targeting you?

M: No. Since I don't have a guaranteed parking space, people might see me park but they have no idea where I live. And I'm not even always on that same street. I don't think it was a hate crime. In any case, a week ago on Monday, I got home from the university and saw a letter from the Los Angeles Police Department saying that my car was in an impound lot in the San Fernando Valley. It was November 1 and I had to get up to Pacoima where this impound lot was. And then I had to pay $696 to get the car out of impound.

A: Who impounded it?

M: When they [the police] find abandoned cars, they impound. The people who stole it parked it on San Fernando Road in Pacoima.

A: Why your car?

M: Who knows? There were fast food boxes in the car, there was syrup spilled on the passenger seat, which I had to clean up. It was messy. Under the seat there were actually a bunch of credit cards for different people, and someone's handicapped placard for their car. So I just want to know what they did with my car while they had it! Who knows what happened. It was weird because there was still gas in the car.

A: Did the police have access to it after? Because they

might have been able to figure it out. I mean, you gave all those cards to the police, right?

M: Oh, I have all the cards in a Ziploc [bag] to take to them because I washed the car on Sunday. The thing is I have to go there during the weekday because they don't have evening hours.

A: Because they could have gotten the fingerprints of the robbers.

M: Well, we'll see what they do with it. I'm going to go drop these cards off at some point next week and just say, "Here it is, do what you need to do." It's very strange because there's a little storage space in the dashboard that's filled with quarters. And the robber didn't take the quarters, but there's another space above it that's filled with receipts that I save from getting gas, and they took the receipts. I wonder what they were thinking. But the engine was fine. The only thing I really had to deal with was replacing the key device because apparently they messed that up. So, I got a new set of keys and then it was fine.

A: Weirdest thing ever. Maybe they used it to commit crimes.

M: Just for a day or two and then they just left it. It's all very strange. But I wasn't really bothered. I mean, it was inconvenient, but compared to other things that I deal with, this was not so bad. And I had the chance to use my bike.

A: And then you revisited public transportation.

M: Yes, that's right. I did that. It works, but it's slow.

A: And you drove that elephant of a van, the Biology department one!

M: I did whatever I had to do, but I'm glad that's all solved.

Interview with Athena Ganchorre—Part 1: I Gave Martina a Chance to Be Herself

Athena Ganchorre and Alicia Partnoy
June 24, 2017

Athena Ganchorre and Martina, along with Aya, right after Martina's gender-confirming surgery, December 2016

A: I would love to hear more about you, Athena. How did you meet Martina?

AG: I met her in 1988, when I was a first-year undergraduate student at UC [University of California] Santa Cruz, and she—then he, Martin Ramirez—was the teaching assistant for my biology class. I thought I wanted to become a park ranger, and I didn't know much about college or careers in science. I didn't know what I was doing, actually.

She asked me, "What do you want to do?" and I responded, "I want to be in a position where I can make positive change." At that point she had this kind of glow in her eyes. Her being an ecologist and sharing similar values about the environment and a love of nature just resonated with me. There was a connection, some trust, some confidence that I would be safe in sharing. I grew up in Washington State, so I was away from home.

A: Where in Washington? I lived in Seattle, it was my first home in the States.

AG: Vashon Island, just off Seattle. You had to take a ferry from Vashon to West Seattle. My brother went to the University of Washington, and I thought, "I can't go anywhere in Washington because I would know somebody." I just didn't want to be near anybody I knew. I wanted to see the world and travel. I was very ambitious and independent. When I arrived at school in Santa Cruz, I quickly realized that there was a lot I didn't know, but I didn't know what I didn't know: I didn't know how to navigate the university.

A: Where did your parents study?

AG: In the Philippines.

A: So in a way you were first generation because they didn't know the system here.

It took me many years to learn how to guide my daughters through the university system in this country. My youngest worked in the spider lab with Martina. That was how I could see more directly her impact on students.

AG: Yeah, her impact on me was quite deep. She immediately asked me if I was interested in going through the Academic Community of Excellence program, as well as being a student teacher. Subsequently she mentored me and asked me to be her teaching assistant. I just couldn't understand her confidence in me. She also recommended me to participate in the MARC Program [Minorities Access Research Careers], an NIH-funded grant. Over the years, I have looked back many times at who has been instrumental in my career path, and it is Martina. I don't even remember how, but I came up with the idea of becoming a park ranger. When I told her that, I think she said, "For example, you could be outside doing these things as a park ranger, or you could be a research scientist." Just having a conversation was in itself a wonderful gift. I didn't feel like the smartest student in the class, but somehow, she made me feel that I had potential, and that's something I've watched her do over and over and over again. I was able to grow and develop an idea of where I wanted to have influence, not only within the social justice framework, but also from the scientific point of view. She taught me all I know, really.

A: What is "all you know?" You went to medical
       school?

AG: That experience as an undergrad—as an ACE
       student, a peer tutor, a teaching assistant, and
       then going into MARC—propelled me to pursue
       a PhD in science. I didn't know then what a PhD
       was. I mean, I knew the words. My grandfather had
       come to the States to do his PhD, and he was on a
       Rockefeller fellowship. He went to Illinois but he
       contracted tuberculosis here in the States, and the
       program sent him back to the Philippines, so he
       couldn't complete his PhD.

A: But wasn't there a treatment for TB then?

AG: Yes, it was treatable, and he had contracted it here.
       I just remember thinking, "This is part of my story
       and I will finish the PhD somehow." I had no idea
       what that really meant. Back then at UC Santa Cruz
       I understood that Martina was a graduate student,
       and somehow a graduate student gets a PhD. I
       watched Martina's career, and she shared with me
       what she was doing. At some point I thought, "This
       is impossible, I don't know if that's something I
       could do." I dropped out of college and didn't go
       back to school until 2006, when I was already 36
       years old.

A: So you did not finish your bachelor's degree in Santa
       Cruz?

AG: Actually I didn't. I dropped out after Martina left. I dropped because I was working and I couldn't make ends meet. I met my former husband, who was getting his PhD, and I got a job at UC Santa Cruz in the Bridge Program for two-year college students going to the university. I was in program and curriculum development to encourage them to continue with their careers. At a point I asked myself, "What's wrong with this? I haven't finished, but I'm very good at supporting students to finish." I also picked up another program for high school students and helped them matriculate in science degrees—biomedical and medical research. My fiancé finished his PhD and I supported and helped him through his career. After that, we went on the PhD academic postdoc life for him, and I deferred my own degree in chemistry. I lived in Japan, in New York, and I finally landed in Arizona. Then I told my husband, "It's my turn, I need to finish my undergrad and I'm going to get my PhD" I don't think he believed me, I really don't think he thought I would follow through.

A: You had a kid?

AG: Yes, he was born right before I started graduate school.

A: I do that all the time! I have a kid from my bachelor's, a kid from my master's degree, and one from my PhD. I managed to complicate my life that way. It can't be easy, so that's what I do.

AG: [*laughs*]

A: When you started your PhD, were you still in contact with Martina?

AG: Yes, once in a while we would get in contact, maybe at a conference. Or I'd hear from other students who had kept in touch with her. I visited her at Bucknell University, and then when she got to Loyola, but prior to Loyola, at Pomona.

A: I think she told me something about going to a pedicure with you in one of those meetings.

AG: Yeah, we also used to go shopping. When I saw her in Bucknell, I took her shopping, and gave her a chance to just feel free and be herself, to express herself openly, without judgment. I don't know how Martina allowed herself to share those things with me, even when I was an undergraduate student. I knew she had had this feeling for a very long time, that she broke off with Rose for a while and tried to live her authentic life. Eventually they got back together, so she had to put it back in the closet. We always had the opportunity to really just speak freely, without worry. I remember coming home from shopping and dropping Martina off when they lived in Santa Cruz. I remember that her wife would be embarrassed. I could see that she was embarrassed—she would say things.

A: To you?

AG: Yeah. She would say things about Martina like, "Oh that's really weird, isn't that really weird?" And I would just go, "Yeah I like it too. I like the dress, I like the panties. Those are nice." And then she would say, "She's got a strange style, she likes these things and I'm just never sure."

   I just ignored her, but it was complicated: I knew Rose because she oversaw the program that funded me as an undergrad. So, there could have been a power issue, but I didn't allow this to interfere. And after that, I developed a friendship with Rose too, because Martina wanted that to happen. Her friends or students became friends with her wife, because Martina has always brought people together. It didn't seem awkward or wrong, but then her wife would disclose how she was uncomfortable with Martina, and at that point, I could only keep neutral. In some cases, if I felt like she was pushing, I would push back and say, "That's just her style. That's what she wants," or "This is who she is," but it was also a little strange to be in that situation because I was a teenager.

A: You must have been amazingly mature, because to be able to navigate that must have been difficult.

AG: I honestly had a hard time understanding how Martina could put up with the things I saw her put up with, and I didn't see everything. I had so much compassion for her. It was not pity, but I observed, and I thought, "How can someone live indoors, not being themselves authentically?" And it was not just about her sexual identity, but multiple layers, as a person of color, and even as a man. I watched how hard she pursued academics and the trials and tribulations associated with that. She has incredibly strong morals and integrity. Her standards are so high for herself and for others. I remember as a student I would tell myself, "Oh my God, I can't possibly reach her ideal."

I remember getting papers back, and everything was red. I used to think, "Oh my God, how will I pass this class?" But she sat with me for hours, helping me do my data or teaching me statistics. I thought, "This is beyond necessary, how can she spend all this time with me?" She taught me how to write scientifically in my undergrad laboratory class. Who takes the time to do that? Then later as a teaching assistant in graduate school, I did the same thing. I would tell my own students, "You're going to walk out of my lab knowing how to write properly. Words mean something, and you have to use precise wording and be accurate in your description."

Digging into Old Teaching Evaluations

Martina Giselle Ramirez and Alicia Partnoy
August 3, 2016

A: Let's take a look at your old teaching evaluations. Oh, you're keeping so many of them! Because they are anonymous, we could use that material for our book easily.

M: Who knows? I would have to go through all these to find something that helps us show students' reactions to my presenting as female.

A: Yeah, but you kept entire packages!

M: The ones from Bucknell will be better. Let's look at them.

A: Were students there more closed-minded? [*laughs*]

M: Well, yes! [*laughs*] So ok, let's see.

A: [*reading evaluations*] "Physiology is very difficult, need a lecture at it." What? Wasn't the student getting lectures? "Organized well but if you're not very familiar with organisms and all sorts of life—" Any professor could get this. "Approachability." That's good. "Instructor's knowledge: They knew something."

M: I'd have to look around for some others.

A: Let's see the comments on this one. "Boring. Too much writing. I don't like seminars." Oh, poor thing! They don't know that those comments are positive for the teacher when she is evaluated by her peers.

M: That's right!

A: This one is interesting. "Learned a lot about spiders, lots of work. Twice as much as any of my other classes." Good! Well, they are all very positive. But these were for your spider class. Maybe other classes got worse evaluations.

In Martina's Bigger World

Susan Christian Goulding , August 28, 2018

SPIDERS IN/AND LITERATURE
FYS 1000.38-CRN 44863 -Fall 2014
Dr. Martina Giselle Ramirez
Office: Seaver 116B • Phone: 338-5120
Martina.Ramirez@lmu.edu

Writing Instructor: Susan Goulding, M.A.
Hours: MW 9:30-11:30; 2:00-2:30; 4:15-5:15

Loyola Marymount University
M/W/F 12-12:50pm
STR 357 / UHall 3244 Language Lab
Office Hours: W 10-11am, 1-2pm, F 1-2pm,
and by appointment.

Office: University Hall 3221
Virtual writing assistance available by
appointment: sgouldin@lmu.edu

Course Description

In this course, we will study the roles spiders play
on the stages of life, as well as in literary works that
have them as characters, themes, or driving
metaphors. Topics for class discussion include:
Environmental preservation, solidarity, political
repression and incarceration, gender stereotyping,
and the writer's role in society. Students will learn
about the lives of spiders, and read narratives by
Native American, U.S and Argentine authors.
Through personal observations of real spiders and
research, participants will reflect and write about
the ways the texts studied in class were informed
by cultural beliefs, scientific knowledge, and/or
misconceptions about spiders. Students will learn
techniques to write and rewrite their essays. As a
class, we will emulate the garden spider *Argiope
aurantia* (the Writing Spider), who daily reworks
her web. This class is co-taught by Professor
Alicia Partnoy.

Student Learning Outcomes

By the end of the semester, successful students
will be able to:

1) Discuss in writing aspects of spider biology,
behavior and ecology.

The syllabus for Spiders in/and Literature, fall semester 2014

Martina Ramirez is a mentor and an inspiration. Yet she offers something more, something that most people, as we travel inside our various bubbles, cannot: a bigger world. She truly opens people's eyes to possibilities of experience that lie beyond the familiar.

In the fall of 2014, I worked as an adjunct writing

teacher at Loyola Marymount University, assisting two professors in their quirky freshman English class which merged spider biology with literature.

I had never before taught at the college level. I knew nothing about the physiology of spiders. And I struggled to envision how such diverse subjects as eight-legged critters and literature would coalesce.

So I was feeling a bit like the proverbial fish out of water when I arrived on campus to plan the syllabus with Martina and her coprofessor, Alicia—our first face-to-face conversation.

We had arranged to meet in Alicia's office. I arrived before Martina made it over from her Spider Lab in the science building.

When Martina walked in and introduced herself, I was momentarily confused. First, I noticed that she was attractive and fashionable, sporting shoulder-length hair, dangly earrings, and a summery dress. But her voice contradicted her feminine appearance.

Of course, my disorientation quickly passed as I realized Martina is transgender.

Somehow, over my five decades, I'd never spent much time with a transgender person. But whatever hyperawareness I initially felt swiftly passed.

Still, on the first day of the semester, I worried about how the incoming freshmen might initially react to a transgender professor. Would they exchange quizzical glances? Would a "jock-ish" boy visibly muffle a snigger? After all, they had been high schoolers just three months before. And, as students at a private Catholic college, many came from sheltered and conservative backgrounds. But as Martina welcomed her class, students seemed utterly unfazed. They were fascinated with the tarantula and other spiders Martina brought along—oohing and laughing and squealing—but displayed no reaction at all to her gender identity. Suddenly, I felt ancient for even imagining any other outcome. This generation has moved far beyond those who came before them in acceptance of their fellow human beings.

Over the next few months, I witnessed Martina and Alicia create a phenomenal class. Students learned about spider-ology one day a week, and on another explored spider-centric short stories and novels, including a charming annotated version of *Charlotte's Web*. The three of us met in Alicia's office once a week, sometimes while nibbling surplus sandwiches we gleefully scavenged from just-emptied conference rooms.

On Halloween day, we threw a spider-themed party for the students and watched the movie *Kiss of the Spider Woman*, having just read the book. It was all great fun.

The final day of the course was held in a lecture hall, where students in panels of three or four presented research papers that, miraculously, bridged the fictional readings with scientific research. The eighteen-year-old freshmen were, basically, defending dissertations—or at least practicing to do so in the future.

Those kids seemed to have matured before my eyes from giddy greenhorns to serious scholars. Martina and Alicia together brought out the best in their charges—each in their own ways, but both with high expectations to which students rose.

Perhaps I digress. This is all to say that Martina is an impressive woman in so many ways: kind, brilliant, warm, wise, and dedicated. Most of all, Martina is courageous in her determination to be herself, and to bring the rest of us along on her journey.

Voice Training: A True Survival Kit

Martina Giselle Ramirez and Alicia Partnoy
July 29, 2016

A: Martina, this is the first time we're recording our talks. Once we put the book together, this conversation might pop up far from its first pages, we'll see. You were just telling me about training your voice and how this device you have in the science lab, the spectrogram, might be useful.

M: On the very first voice training CD they suggest you get one of these devices to use when commuting in your car, or even when you're hiking, because you can speak into it and play it back later. When you hold the speaker near the spectrogram, it will give you a plot for what your voice looks like. For example, I ran the spectrogram software while playing back Michelle Obama's Democratic Convention Speech to see where her pattern was in terms of frequency. Then I just spoke into it to see where I fit in. I haven't fully figured out all the details, but it is really cool.

A: You must be tired. How long did you do that for?

M: I did it for over an hour. They have a video demonstration with a person modeling what you're supposed to do. They say, "Feel your throat as you're doing this," "Say these letters." "Try to do this and that." And then they say, "Okay, hear yourself trying it." So you start to work different sets of muscles, and once you've done it for a while, you realize, "Oh my gosh, I'm actually getting kind of hot, this is like a workout!" [*laughs*]

They want you to use different muscle sets, something you never normally do. They have you do a sort of gargling. They have you clear your throat to say different letters and they give you specific instructions, like "Try it deep." "Try to make your throat as wide as you can." "Say these letters." This CD is pretty long, so I haven't gotten through all the different stages, I've only done it one night so far.

A: It reminds me of when I did a seminar for faculty members here, and a professor came to teach us about voice relaxation. It was fascinating because he made me read in Spanish and in English, and he said my voice is completely different when I read in English. It sounds like a child's voice, and more stressed. He showed me the muscles I need to relax. The truth is that he was right, I'm always stressed, fearing that I'll mispronounce words in English.

M: So you tense up.

A: Yeah. I'm not rationally scared of speaking English, but he made me aware that my throat does not relax when I do it in public. Now, let me ask you a question that might sound stupid: Why do you feel the need to do this voice training?

M: Well, when people in my situation call an 800 number to place an order, the rule of thumb is you're asking: When will they stop assuming that you're a male? Because there is an operator at whatever company, and you're trying to place an order with your credit card, and depending on how you sound, people will immediately tag you as female or male. In other words, the idea is to not be categorized as a guy just on your voice.

A: Wow, now I understand why the program is called "survival kit." I was surprised to see that label on the product.

M: Right! But some people don't bother with this. It's not simple to do, it takes a lot of dedication. If you have money, you can just hire a voice coach, but for people who have fewer resources, this is a fifty-dollar set of CDs that you can do on your own. Clearly, when you think of the people that the media spotlights, you assume that they have enough money for surgeries, as well as the ability to hire a voice coach. There are even surgeries to change the length of your vocal chords. The idea is that if you have the money, you can find the experts.

A: But you must be willing to go under the knife too.

M: Of course! Most trans people spotlighted in the media have a lot of money. The only individuals they portray as the public face for the trans world are those with access to all the resources. The reality is that most people in my situation never get the spotlight. I used to weigh over two hundred pounds, and that made me aware of how things play out when you're big, too. We live in a world where there is a fatness phobia, where you seldom see in fashion magazines or *Sports Illustrated* a model who is not super crazy thin.

A: Or they feature other people just as tokens, right?

M: Indeed! The idea is that you're not a virtuous woman unless you've done whatever it takes to have this perfect slim body; you're not a serious woman unless you achieve that kind of body, *and* we are going to give you grief if you're not that way. If you look at all the body sizes around you, does that mean these people are lazy and not serious? Does it mean that we have to just write off everybody who doesn't have this particular set of features?

A: Isn't it also true that when glamorous trans people appear in the media, we see them only as a finished product—we don't see the process?

M: Right. For people like me, the implication is that everything is perfect for them and that unless you're like them, you're lesser in some way, shape, or form.

Therefore, you should get your act together and try to be like them. Can't we be really accepting of people? To me, this world of gender identity transition shares many of the issues we see regarding body shape—and neither is right [*voice breaks*].

A: You have gone through so much, Martina.

M: For me this is very personal. Most of my life I knew who I really was, but I was in a situation where I couldn't be open or expressive about it. But that didn't stop me from seeing how all the silliness around me played out. I could see relationships in my family where male dominance was displayed, where spouses were not treated correctly, yet people accepted it. They would tell themselves, "Oh this is the way the world is." I knew it wasn't right, and it was personal for me. Because people thought I was just a guy. [*sniffles*] I never was!

Hiding for Tenure at a Religious School

Martina Giselle Ramirez, May 26, 2017

Back in the '90s, when I taught at four different schools, I used to read *The Chronicle of Higher Education*. One day, around the year 1995, I found an article about a transgender faculty member at the University of San Francisco. I considered that article seriously noteworthy because the general assumption in those days was that if a transgender person taught at any religiously affiliated school, the environment for them was going to be hard—it was going to prevent that person from succeeding in academia. My colleagues at that time were genuinely surprised by that case at USF. They would say things like, "A religiously affiliated school has hired somebody trans in a tenure track position? What were they thinking?" Later, as a new tenure track faculty member at Loyola Marymount University, it was a wakeup call. It made me more aware of the potential problems I might have encountered if I had presented as a woman. That led me to put away who I was for eleven years: I did not want to risk my chances of getting tenure and promotion.

Becoming Martina Giselle

Martina Giselle Ramirez and Alicia Partnoy
August 24, 2016

A: How did you start thinking of yourself as Martina?

M: In 2014, when I went through the process of having my legal name changed, I didn't have the choice to go very far from Martin Gabriel because I had published many years of scientific papers under that name. I didn't want to go totally different and be Sarah, for example. If I had to just put an A at the end, fine. I also thought of ending it with an E instead. With the middle name, because many academic papers just list the middle initial, there was more latitude. I just wanted to keep the first letter the same, and that actually was way more open and fun. I read lists of baby names starting with G online.

A: Giselle is beautiful.

M: It took a while to get there. I tried Gabrielle for a while, and it was fine, but it didn't sound right when you said the full name. And then, one morning when I was getting ready to go work out, this Giselle name popped into my head, which sounded great.

A: You were not living by yourself then?

M: No, I wasn't. So, as soon as I got to work, I looked up "Giselle" online and saw that many cultures have that name with different spellings. It was cool, so the next thing I did was to go on Facebook and search for people with the same first and middle name, and oh my! There were other people out there, mostly in Venezuela.

A: With your same name?

M: Yes, the same first and middle name [*laughs*]. I found like five or six women. People have asked, "Suppose you didn't have that constraint on your first name. What would you have done?" Good question. I don't know. Since I believed it was not going to be an option, I never gave it much thought.

A: Your old name, Martin, did it come from somebody in the family?

M: It was my dad's name. And my old middle name was my first name when they got me from the orphanage. At the maternity hospital, I was Gabriel Arellano.

That was my orphan name, for a nine-month-old little baby sitting there.

A: So you know your birth name!

M: When my parents told me they had adopted me from St. Anne's Maternity House, I went there and got what records they had, and this is what I remember. They had a record listing my biological parents and their background.

A: So you do have some information! When we started to record our talks, you said something about wanting to know more about them.

M: I know my parents were from Puerto Rico, but I don't have their names.

A: But you have that last name, so that's a good place to start. I'm a little bit of a detective. My mom would say, "Look, so and so and I haven't been in touch for fifty years. Can you find her?" And most of the times I would find the person.

M: Keep in mind this was in January 1981. So I have to try to remember where I kept that information, or if my mom kept it.

A: I'm surprised that you remember your biological parents' last name but you have not searched for them online or anything. Maybe after we publish this book, some relatives from Puerto Rico will reach out to you.

M: That would be wonderful! I'd especially like to know if I have siblings, and if so, hopefully get in contact with them.

Reflecting on Trans Narratives and Future Leadership Roles

Martina Giselle Ramirez, May 26, 2017

A few months ago, my health insurance, Kaiser Permanente, invited a group of transgender people to be part of a panel on our experiences. The audience wrote questions for us, and one that I found very interesting was the request to recommend a book. It was a great opportunity to discuss our book project and to elaborate on the fact that not many trans narratives shared our approach.

Trans narratives tend to present the transgender person's story in the following terms: Here's my life after transition, here's my life before transition—a terrible existence that must be put in a closet and forgotten because it was embarrassing. That's not my reality. I am not downhearted about my life prior to transitioning because it was a life spent working for the poor and underserved, for first-generation students, low-income students, LGBTQ+ students, for people of color who, like me, did not get enough love in the world. Those are all my people. Had I gone to my grave without transitioning, I would not have gone thinking that my life had been a big zero.

I told the audience at that Kaiser Permanente panel that I had bigger issues to push forward, and those were worth more to me than my personal experience. Even though I love being authentically who I am, if that had not happened for me in a tangible way, as long as I could have still pushed for these other issues, I could be certain that my life had left a positive legacy.

I also reflected on the idea that people have multiple identities. In my case, I used to be plus sized (I weighed over two hundred pounds), and so I experienced how people gave me grief because of my size. For example, when I was an altar server at the church, one day the other servers bugged me so much about how tightly my cassock fit that we got into a fight in the anteroom behind the altar, unseen by the priest. I also had to endure discrimination for being a first-generation college student, from a low-income background, and a person of color. Thus, being trans was just one of my identities. And the truth is that I have not seen any narratives out there that communicate these multiple experiences together.

And the other issue with current trans narratives is the issue of the way transness is presented in the media. People think of figures like Caitlyn Jenner—wealthy individuals who can access all the technological advances to transform their bodies and always look stunning. The impression I get from such people seems to be, "I made it because I'm super awesome," and then they ride off into the sunset, and it is just about them.

The reality is that most trans people do not have such resources or opportunities. Now that I'm personally at the point where I am just checking boxes on what I'm doing for my transition, now that this process is just fine-tuning, I'm thinking about what I can do to support people out there who do not have resources, who do not have Kaiser coverage, who are in communities that hate them, in family settings where they are detested, where they endure realities that drive so many trans people to be depressed or attempt suicide.

I'm now trying to think of an avenue to work for the well-being of other people in this world who are trans, but who don't have access to resources or to environments that accept them. Is there some nonprofit that I can join? If not, do I need to form one? I realize this is not something you do as one person; the point is to find people similarly inclined to make progress. For example, I've always admired the way that Gustavo Dudamel came to LA to direct the Los Angeles Philharmonic orchestra, and at the same time he created the Youth Orchestra Los Angeles (YOLA). This orchestra has provided quality music education to thousands of children from underserved communities.

Another interesting example is Bill Gates. Before Microsoft, he was a normal, techy person, and then he became a billionaire. So, what did he do? He created The Bill and Melinda Gates Foundation. He is out there giving away billions to do good. Now we have trans people who are similarly at a pinnacle. I wonder if they think about reproducing in the trans world what Bill Gates is doing in the philanthropic world?

For example, there are some countries where if you are transgender, you are killed in terrible ways. If I had the resources, I would mobilize successful transgender icons to help fix those problems. I'm always thinking about ways to get involved. This is part of the reason for my interest in leadership in higher education. If I serve as a dean or in other high-level administrator positions, I could eventually transition my career into a nonprofit foundation. I would love to work for a foundation that is concerned about transness as well as social justice issues of equity and access. For me, that is the next phase in my professional life—leadership at a high level and helping others via nonprofit work.

This was all part of the conversation in that panel at Kaiser Permanente, but I did not recommend any books. I just told them: "Be aware when you look at these narratives—you might see some of the elements I am discussing." We need people who offer more than the glitzy trans experience. Maybe that is some people's reality, but it is not mine, and I believe many trans people feel as I do.

Christine Jorgensen's Parents Say She Is So Happy Now

. . . .

Martina Giselle Ramirez and Alicia Partnoy
August 24, 2016

A: I see many little pieces of paper sticking out of your copy of [transgender pioneer] Christine Jorgensen's book![7] Let's go through it to see how her experience back then resonates with yours today.

M: For example, here's one statement that shows her faith in the medical profession, and then she mentions a letter to her friends where she discusses how if her surgery is successful, it will be meaningful to thousands. She writes, "I am not alone in this affliction. I think we, the doctors and I, are fighting this the right way to make the body fit the soul rather than vice versa."[8] Those words struck me because I never thought my own transition was going to be just about me.

A: Who would know that some health insurances policies pay for this, unless they do research or read our book?

M: Right. However, those policies don't pay for all of the things that wealthy people can have done. Christine Jorgensen also realized at some point that being out in the public eye made her a role model for people. Of course, she didn't like the way her personal letters were leaked to newspapers. But she became aware that she was an example for people like her, an example that there was happiness on the other side [after transitioning], there was a better life on the other side.

A: Because she could have thought, "I'm an entertainer, I'm doing this for myself. This is fame for me." But obviously something else drove her.

M: There are many examples from her life: the fact that she went on the college lecture circuit after her entertaining days, that she cooperated with famous doctors who were trying to get the gender-confirming medical field together. She didn't have to do those things. She could have just made it about her personal success story. In my case, I've never thought of myself as an activist.

A: You were very low key in activism even before, as a Latino professor here. You always supported activist students, but were not the face for activism yourself.

M: Right! Another interesting fact in Jorgensen's book is that she wore male clothes until the state department approved her passport with her female gender and her female name. Then, and only then, she made the move to wear female clothes in public. And she talks about making her own outfits with a sewing machine!

A: And that was in the 1950s?

M: Indeed. She says, "I've been preparing for that time for several months, and I've gotten some patterns and fabrics to try my hand at sewing. I have little or no money to spend for readymade things."[9]

A: It's an echo of your own experience.

M: Well, where do I go all the time? I shop at Goodwill, or my students, their mothers, or my friends give me bags of stuff. But there's something else here, which she mentions. She talks about one of her first days at a beauty salon. She goes with a friend, and they get a manicure, a facial, all these things. When they leave, as they're walking to a park, she's shocked and moved to laughter by a wolf call in her direction.

A: [laughs]

M: The reason I bring that up is—I haven't been cat called, but when I walk along 80th Street, guys driving by sometimes turn and look at me. That makes me do a double take: "Wait, what? Who are they looking at?" [laughter]

"Oh, they're looking at you!" I realize. "Wow, this really happens!"

But going back to that chapter of Jorgensen's book, she says that she had a joyful and busy summer after her surgery, and she found acceptance and felt comfortable and happy. Christine shares that those feelings seemed to be contagious and that the people working with her enjoyed her company. I can relate. Not that I was down in the doldrums before, but that whole business of contagious happiness, I know what she's talking about. It is also interesting to see the letter that Christine's mom wrote to her friends, Dr. Joe Angelo and his wife, thanking them effusively for "helping her find her true self, she is so happy now."[10] This is her mom in the 1950s!

A: She speaks for both herself and father?

M: I gather that her father never flipped out.

A: There's nothing about him being shocked or opposed?

M: Not that I saw. So, I was just struck by that, because clearly, not everybody who goes through this experience has parents like them. To have a parent step up that way, with the attitude of, "You're still my child and you are happier now." It's amazing.

A: Even when her parents had to endure the harassment of the media!

M: She talks about reporters parked outside their house, hounding them constantly. When they tried to get the mail, reporters would stick microphones in their faces. They had to slip out and be incognito if they wanted to go shopping. They had to be really creative to just try to live a normal life. Christine realized her own life had been pretty hectic since the surgery, too. She was on a long plane flight across the Atlantic and used her time alone to reflect on her life. She was happy about her choices, and confident that her loneliness and fear would become a thing of the past.[11]

A: This is on pages 164 and 165. And the connection with God is there too?

M: Yes, she mentions all these reporters wanting to know about her business, but they never really asked her about her faith. They were all focused on titillating questions like, "What do you sleep in? Do you sleep in a nightie? Are you dating somebody? Are you going to marry a guy?" Just all that tabloid craziness. Didn't those journalists ever think of more relevant questions, like how she felt in that big personal journey and if faith was important in her life? It didn't occur to them that maybe Christine was thinking about her relationship with God and how this was part of a journey to be truer to the Creator. That struck me.

A: Did you finish the book?

M: Yes! See the little bookmarks sticking out on pages 296 and 297? Here she reflects on the whole idea of transsexualism, and how finally it was openly discussed in newspapers and magazines. She says that the press took notice that John Hopkins University in the US was performing gender-confirming surgeries.

A: They must have been much more expensive than the one she had in Denmark.

M: I suppose. This is 1966, fourteen years after her own surgery. She talks about the impact of an article in the front page of the *New York Times* about the gender identity clinic and the two surgeries "quietly" performed at the renowned Johns Hopkins Hospital in September and October of 1966. She transcribes the long article, and she says that they still received some pushback, but at least it was out in the open. She also writes, "If I proved to be a catalyst in some of these events, I have seldom been aware of it. Never at any time have I regarded myself as a crusader or rebel fighting for a cause, except on a few occasions and those only when my personal freedoms were threatened. I've never been very good at carrying banners into battle . . . In essence, it was a search for dignity and the right to live in freedom and happiness."[12] I can identify with her in "not carrying a banner into battle."

My Dinner with Christine Jorgensen

Martina Giselle Ramirez, October 12, 2016

In summer 2016, I was contacted by Joseph Wakelee-Lynch, editor of *LMU Magazine*. He invited me to be part of a piece that was being planned for an upcoming issue. The question he posed to me and several others was: "If you could have dinner and conversation with anyone in the past, who would you pick and why?" Each response was to be brief, and would be accompanied in the magazine by a professionally drawn, black and white portrait of the dinner guest. Once the responses and portraits were ready for publication, all the faculty members to be featured in the piece were invited to an outdoor dinner party near the Bird Nest at Loyola Marymount University, resulting in the image that accompanies my text below.

Christine Jorgensen, an ex-G.I., became nationally known after undergoing gender-confirming surgery in Denmark in 1952. When I was in elementary school, I read "*Christine Jorgensen: A Personal Autobiography*,"

Martina at the My Dinner With outdoor meal, October 2016. Photo by Jon Rou.

a milestone in my journey of self-discovery. This summer, I reread Christine's book and was struck by the relevance of many of her experiences for contemporary trans issues. For example, Christine once dealt with lack of bathroom access when she was barred by police from using public women's restrooms in Washington, D.C. Moreover, while she regularly dealt with often lurid questions about intimate details of her anatomy and personal life following her return to the United States, no one ever asked about the relationship between her faith and her gender transition. Thus, I'd love to have dinner with Christine to hear her perspective on transness then and now, given her role as a trailblazer for we transwomen of today.

Amending My Birth Certificate

Martina Giselle Ramirez and Alicia Partnoy
August 24, 2016

A: Oh! The State of California gives you an example of how to amend your birth certificate!

M: The instructions say, "Fill it out exactly like we have. So here is your old male information, here is your new female information. Here is the reason." Then if you change your name, you have to give them the court order document that changes your name. I just have to follow the template and type everything. The cool thing is that one of my students is a notary, and I had to have one of these documents notarized, so she did it!

A: So, you amend your actual birth certificate? For a woman who gets married and wants to use her husband's name, she just changes her name, but here you amend the birth record?

M: One of the things that I had to find for this was a copy of my original birth certificate. I'm curious because I imagine that they're going to send this back with the details changed. So, we'll see. Actually, I didn't have a copy and I had to first get a copy because my mom had it.

A: You were born in February. Me too.

M: What day?

A: The seventh.

M: I want to get this mailed off before school starts. They made it much simpler because it's just a twenty-three-dollar check and these documents, and you just have to send them in.

A: And they give you all these directions because these forms are so hard to figure out.

M: I know. Once I get this back, I'll be able to change my passport. Social security has my correct name, but they won't change my gender until the birth record is changed.

   That's why I bookmarked the page [in Christine Jorgensen's autobiography] where Jorgensen tries to get married and it's like, "Wait, you don't have the correct birth certificate, stop."

A: She would solve that, and she would overcome any accusations of trying to do things women do, like going to the women's bathroom.

M: It's like when the inspector of the police Morals Squad in Washington tells her something that could be understood as, "Hold your pee while you're in Washington DC, good luck," and she replies, with her characteristic aplomb and sense of humor, that she would "try very hard to contain" herself.[13]

Bathroom Blues

. . . .

Martina Giselle Ramirez, August 5, 2016

In the summer of 2010, the very first summer I presented as female all the time, I started using a restroom down the hall from my office in the Seaver Science Hall at Loyola Marymount University. I didn't know how I would be treated if I went into the women's restroom at that point, so I just kept using the men's bathroom for a time. Over the summer, I was doing research with students when, one day, the college dean, who hardly ever visited me, came to see me in the Spider Lab. He wanted to talk in private, so I told the students to keep working on sexing spider babies while the dean and I went to my office and closed the door.

He then told me that some faculty in my building were annoyed because I was using the men's restroom down the hall. He didn't give me any names, though I certainly had an idea of who they might have been. Then the dean proceeded to share with me that he had been the chairperson of an engineering department before coming to

LMU and that back then, one of his faculty members had transitioned from male to female. He told me he had tried to be supportive of that person, to defend them amidst mixed reactions within the department, where some people were accepting, while others saw it as terrible.

While I didn't mention this to the dean, I was not surprised by this reaction from some colleagues in the sciences. Since women have traditionally been underrepresented in the faculty of science fields, including at LMU, it made sense that some colleagues might be disturbed by my crossing of the gender divide. But I just thought "whatever," and started going downstairs to use an all-gender restroom in the basement, which had been there for years to serve basement classrooms and offices. Once my transition was far enough along and I'd had enough hair removal on my face, I started using the women's restroom, and it was all fine.

At our meeting, the dean had said that he would do what he could to make sure that my experience at LMU was appropriate. I didn't know exactly what he meant, and that was how things were left. Every year there is an award given to a science and engineering professor for student and faculty research, the Rudenica Award. In 2012, when I went to the ceremony presenting as female, I was stunned to find out that I was the winner and that the prize was a $3,000 check and a giant inscribed plaque. It definitely would have been interesting to know what kind of conversations went on in the selection committee convened to choose the winner for the award since they did not have to select a trans woman as winner but did so anyway.

Bathroom Laws

Martina Giselle Ramirez and Alicia Partnoy
August 4, 2016

M: When I came out, there was a wedding reception for one of my former students that I didn't attend because I didn't know what the bathroom situation was going to be. I was really bummed that I didn't go, but—

A: These are the kinds of everyday issues that people didn't use to think about, but now they're in the papers. I'll send you the link to this article. Don't these people have something better to do with their lives than just preventing kids from going to the bathroom?

M: "Supreme Court Grants Emergency Order to Block Transgender Student in Virginia from Using Boys' Restroom,"[14] August 3. I had not read this article.

A: It was in yesterday's *Los Angeles Times*. It's about all the legal issues and what the schools and judges are discussing. Out of politeness towards the other justices, this one decides to go with them because schools are on vacation, and he says they will revisit the issue later. Meanwhile, it is a setback for human rights.

M: So they're playing games with the fact that the court has only eight people instead of nine.

A: I don't agree with this justice deciding to align with the rest out of so-called "politeness." What about being polite to the people in the world outside of your court?

M: And when you look at the people who push these bathrooms laws, what they are saying is that they're trying to avoid men sneaking into the women's restroom to do sexual activities with them. The modus operandi is, "Let's create this confusion and then let's go create all these laws to make life tough for those we don't respect."

Anticipating My Gender-Confirming Surgery

Martina Giselle Ramirez and Alicia Partnoy
November 11, 2016

A: We are barely six weeks away from your surgery, and I wonder if you have had time to think about it in this frenzy of preparations, classes, duties. Do you ever think about your life afterwards?

M: Since we talked last month, there's been this flurry of activity. Yesterday the doctors who'll perform the surgery in Arizona needed a clearance letter from my local doctor confirming I was ready. They also needed an electrocardiogram. I had seen my doctor here back in August, and then in October, but I got an email with a list of the stuff they still needed at the hospital. So, I've been scrambling around, and I had to get on the doctor's calendar again. At the appointment, the local doctor composed the letter right when I was sitting there, she took the EKG, and then she emailed me a copy. So the people in Arizona are apparently happy.

A: So things are on track for your surgery in December!

M: Yes! There are two nurses with Kaiser Permanente that coordinate the details for all the transition cases. They divide their patients alphabetically. One takes care of the top of the list, and the other the rest of the patients. My nurse contacted me about this letter they needed, and she also said, "Oh, by the way, we also need you to have an appointment with the psychologist you saw a couple of years ago, so that he can pass judgment that you're ok."

A: Where is this psychologist?

M: He's over here, he's close.

A: Oh, good, he hasn't moved.

M: But I had to get in his calendar! So I emailed him asking for his earliest available appointment, and he emails me back, "I have November 30." But the nurse said that it was less than a month before my surgery— not soon enough. So I was online again with the psychologist, and he looked around and, "Oh, there's this cancellation October 31 at nine a.m." So I went to see him that day, and he wrote the letter right there while I was sitting in his office. Fine, another thing off the list. But then the nurse called me and said, "You also need a current blood test for your endocrinologist to look at your hormone levels."

A: But couldn't they have told you all these things before?

M: I know! Go figure. I don't like surprises. I wonder why they didn't tell me all this in advance so I could have scheduled all those things? In any case, the blood test happened on Monday this week. I emailed the nurse, "Do you have everything? Is there anything else I need to do?" I also emailed the people in Arizona, "You got any more stuff? Are you happy now?" Nobody has said anything so far, so I guess they're happy. There was all this craziness, all these gymnastics with scheduling.

A: People assume that you don't have a life, you don't work—

M: Of course, and then I had to cancel classes. These people have their calendars, I can't get into their calendar . . . It just worked out that they had cancellations. It was just too much drama!

My Messages at Lavender Graduation

Martina Giselle Ramirez, August 3, 2016

I was invited to give a keynote speech at the Lavender Graduation, an event at Loyola Marymount University to honor the LGBTQ+ graduates and their families. As I often do, I showed the audience a PowerPoint presentation with pictures about my life and the many students I have mentored all these years. I finished with an encouraging message: I reassured them there was scientific proof that they are prepared to succeed in life.

I shared with them a study in which the Gallup organization and Purdue University's social scientists looked at responses from thirty thousand graduates who were asked about five indicators of well-being.[15] Their conclusion was that students with encouraging faculty mentors had increased possibilities for success. The other two positive factors were having an internship or a job, and having been engaged on an academic project for at least one semester. Then I mentioned the other indicator the measured: engagement in meaningful work, jobs that were more than just collecting pay.

I asked students to raise their hands if these indicators were present in their own experiences in college, and I listed each one. Once the students could see that their hands were raised many times, I told them, "Usually when people say that you are going to do well in life, they do not show any evidence, and you are just supposed to trust them. Your experience at our university is already giving you contact with a lot of these experiences that—we know from data—will help you do well in life. So, remain calm—I have evidence. I am a scientist, so you know I must have data. You will be okay after graduation."

These were some of my reflections that day: "Someday you're going to be a professional, and whatever job you have, you'll be likely to attend more than your share of meetings. Meetings are where policies are made, where issues are discussed, and where you have a chance to advocate for the way things should be done. As you become a person with influence, take time to reflect on what to do with that influence. Father Greg Boyle encourages us to 'make the circle of compassion bigger so that no one is left standing outside.'[16]

"You'll have a chance to do that in your workplace and in the world, to make the community more welcoming and inclusive. As you may have noticed, the current political season is filled with worrying signs. Currently, people are working to cement differences rather than to unite the increasingly diverse American citizens. Omid Safi, a blogger I follow who directs the Islamic Studies Center at Duke University, posted about this political realm that tries to divide people. He remarked that when we allow hatred or venom toward one of us Muslims, Jews, or gays, we all go down together. As Martin Luther King Jr. used to say, 'Either we go up together or we go down together.'"

I then told students, "Try to make the world you move in, your workplace, but also the larger public space, more open and accepting of people. There are examples right in our city: the African American and Japanese American communities in Southern California who worked together and got along over the decades. They cooperated at key times because they were both at the butt end of discrimination. I just read Scott Kurashige's *The Shifting Grounds of Race*, about Black and Japanese Americans' joint contributions to Los Angeles, and I am currently reading Shana Bernstein's *Bridges of Reform: Interracial Civil Rights Activism in Twentieth-Century Los Angeles*. Bernstein expands the picture to include Mexican Americans and Jews. She tells you how over the 1920s, '30s, '40s, and '50s, these four groups that were sitting at the receiving end of discriminatory practices learned to cooperate and to work together.

"Some people think it is so hard to work with others, but we have examples of diverse communities that figured out how to work together. We don't have to create this out of thin air. Let us examine some examples from our times.

"You might be aware that North Carolina passed the absurd HB2 bill, the 'bathroom bill.'[17] Director of Duke University's Islamic Center Omid Safi posted in his blog: 'Don't be silent.' Safi talks about how boycotts were used in the South, and in South Africa, the West Bank, and North Carolina, and are an effective strategy. But, he says, they are not the only strategy. Whatever you do, do not be silent. Don't grow up to be an individual just concerned about people of your own skin color or your own background and who ignores the suffering or issues of others.

"When you're growing up, the generation before you is passing the leadership baton. This is the world you will inherit as leaders. It is a very beautiful place, but it is also imperfect. There's poverty, injustice, inequality, and no lack of things to fix. Whether this beautiful world gets better or not depends on you. This Jesuit Ignatian education has instilled in you an ethical framework, values, a sense that your life is about more than just you. Take what you have learned and put it into action, because that's the only way this beautiful world is going to become better for the people who live here, and also for the critters. I always had these goals in life, and now, after eleven years of not being open about who I am, in 2010 I just had enough with pretending. I started being fully myself again. I would always say, 'Do whatever it takes to be true to your dream.' And now, you can see that I am walking my talk."

Wear a Bra, No Problem

· ·

Martina Giselle Ramirez and Alicia Partnoy
July 28, 2017

A: [Trans icons] Christine Jorgensen and Janet Mock talk in their books about how they both self-medicated with hormones. Janet says that's the case with many people. Back then, Christine was a genius. She didn't have any training as a biologist but she researched the effects of hormones and decided to self-medicate! You are a scientist, so did you ever think of taking hormones on your own?

M: I never thought about it because there was never money for anything outside the basic things. It was crazy dragging a family across the country for six years on wimpy salaries, and barely any relocation funds, or none at all. I read about what people had done, but it was like, "Am I going to be able to pay for hormone treatments? I don't think so."

A: You began your hormone treatment later in life, like a couple of years ago, right?

M: In 2014.

A: There is a page in *Redefining Realness* where Janet Mock writes about the first pill that she took. It's a whole description. Do you remember your first pills?

M: I saved the bottles of my original set of meds and I took a picture. I think it might be in a Facebook post, but yes, I remember the day.

A: Was that when we were teaching together?

M: No, that was spring 2014, and we taught together that fall. I have my originals up there [*pointing to a line of blue prescription containers on a top shelf in her office*].

A: Do you remember the color of the first pill?

M: It was blue.

A: They are all the same color?

M: I think the sizes are different, so let me see [*reaching up to get the bottles and opening them*]. This is one milligram. This is 9/24/14, 7/24/14. I'd have to look around.

A: That's ok, this is more than what I thought I was going to get. [*laughs*]

M: I've got my records of dosages online. At some point they added this, the methylprogesterone. But the other thing that started basically very early on is this anti-testosterone thing, because they have to stop the testosterone. This is the testosterone blocker that destroys it or competes with it.

A: So, they are up there in that blue glass tray—is that from the hospital?

M: No, that's a graduation gift from a student.

A: And also up on that shelf, there is that box with a big plane that needs to be assembled.

M: I've had that since undergrad days. I bought that in the South Bay.

A: Oh wow, those pills have been on that shelf since 2014!

M: Yes, by the Enya CDs.

A: When did you start feeling results, feeling different?

M: In June. I began to take the pills in May, and in one month I started to see something. I work out every day at the YMCA, and at some point in June I started noticing that I had nipple sensitivity. And I realized,

"Wait, I need to wear a sports bra!" It was getting uncomfortable because I'm bouncing up and down on the elliptical machine and it's like, "Oh, God." Basically, when I started, the nipple tips were super sensitive, and as time went on it just kind of moderated itself. So initially I was like, "Oh my God, they're really tender." But I said to myself, "Wear a bra, no problem."

Coaching Students for Stardom in STEM Careers

Martina Giselle Ramirez, Summer 2015

*I*n 2015 I wrote a proposal of an essay piece for potential submission to a SoTL (Scholarship of Teaching
and Learning) journal. My contribution would outline
the steps I had taken to forge a career focused on students
rather than on myself. It would be interspersed with
vignettes concerning my development as a transgender
academic and administrator (when I first presented as
female at UCSC in the late 1980s; being out as trans
while a faculty member at four universities in the 1990s;
enduring eleven years of secrecy while pursuing tenure
and promotion at Loyola Marymount University, and
coming out in 2010 and subsequently transitioning).
Below is the text of my proposal.

As an adopted, first-generation Latina from the low socioeconomic community of Pomona who enrolled at Loyola
Marymount University in fall 1977, I arrived with low

cultural capital—"the knowledge, skills, education, and other advantages a person needs to make the educational system a comfortable, familiar environment in which he or she can succeed easily."[18]

For students like me, learning how to assess the features of and opportunities available at what is a culturally and physically different place is no easy task, one that can easily compromise one's ability to realize the hoped-for benefits of the college experience.

However, thanks to two factors that were critical in facilitating my success in life—mentorship and engagement with faculty in their scholarly work—I continued my education through the doctorate, which led to my faculty experiences of the last twenty-five years. Sadly, a number of peers in my biology major cohort did not similarly persist in the major, as they either changed to non-STEM [science, technology, engineering, and math] majors or transferred to other institutions. This was especially true for those who were women and/or from underrepresented backgrounds. While their particular reasons for doing so were likely as variable as they were, one potential factor in this attrition by gender and ethnicity was the fact the Seaver College of Science and Engineering faculty was almost entirely male—there was only one woman—and almost entirely Caucasian.

During the fall of 1977, the professor for my freshman calculus class was Jacqueline Dewar, one of the first women hired for a tenure-track slot in the college. Thereafter, I had only male professors for the balance of my college curriculum (courses in biology, chemistry, and physics) at LMU. To me, it made sense that if a student seldom, if ever, saw a faculty member who looked like

Jacqueline Dewar and Martina, October 2018

them in their STEM courses and majors, they might not necessarily feel inspired to persist, especially when in classes for other majors, they did see faculty members they could relate to in gender and/or ethnicity. This realization is a key reason I first considered a faculty career myself, since I knew that such a role would allow me to be a change agent in this area, someone who could boost the representation of women and underrepresented people in STEM, one person at a time.

As the first step in my journey toward faculty-hood, I joined the PhD program in biology at the University of California, Santa Cruz in fall 1981. As I moved through courses and research activities in the ensuing years, I encountered sometimes subtle messages to the effect that I was being trained to take up a faculty position at a research university, and that to do otherwise once I had my PhD would mark me as a "loss to the profession." Indeed, Clark Kerr noted at the time that the intense focus on research at UC and similar institutions had given rise to the "veneration of the non-teacher," with the outcome that "the higher a professor's standing, the less he or she has to do with students!"[19]

Given my prior experiences with faculty members who actively facilitated my success in academics—and in life—the supposed virtue of shunning students so as to have a robust research career did not sit well with me, so I actively resisted the pressures to conform, both at UC Santa Cruz and beyond. Instead, I built a career focused on fostering the representation of women and underrepresented people in STEM, an endeavor which has been highly successful. From 2011 to 2016, sixty-nine students in the LMU Spider Lab gave conference presentations. Of these, sixty-five were women and thirty-nine were members of groups that are underrepresented in STEM fields. Of the sixty-six students who are now alumni, all have gone on to graduate and professional programs and/ or to employment in areas relevant to their STEM majors.

A Surprising Experience

· ·

Martina Giselle Ramirez and Alicia Partnoy
July 25, 2017

M: I come to the Life Science building [at Loyola Mary-mount University] every Sunday. When I'm there, most of the time, one of the facilities people comes in to mop and wax the floors. He's got this big machine. I see him pretty much every week. Two Sundays ago, it was a really warm day so I had stayed home. I work out on Sunday, I go wash the car, and I go to school at about 1 o'clock. I'm wearing this swim dress because it's super-hot in my apartment, and my car is on the street for hours and you get into it and it's like an oven on wheels. So, I walk in and he says, "My! You look nice today!" [*laughs*]

A: [*laughs*]

M: And then he came up about half an hour later. Knock, knock, knock.

A: At your office door?

M: Yes! And he's like, "Oh, I just wanted to say I hope you weren't taken aback by my words." And I didn't tell him, "No, you actually made my day in a big way!" I had to laugh and say, "No problem!" I explained that I have this ancient car with no air conditioning, so I try to wear airy clothes on these days, since my car is sitting in the sun until the afternoon when I finally get into it to come to school.

A: So you had to explain why you were a sexy professor.

M: Yes. I just had to laugh because, "Wait, you just got a compliment, oh my God!"

A: You don't feel objectified?

M: You always wonder in my situation whether people look at you in the same way that they look at other women. Not that those comments are good things all the time, but if you've never had any of this coming your way your whole life, when you do, it's like, "Wow! What is this? That was really neat."

A: Janet Mock in her *Redefining Realness* book analyzes that sometimes these comments objectify you, but sometimes they are an acknowledgment that you are beautiful, so they can be reaffirming.

Some Entertaining Pre- and Postsurgery Instructions

Martina Giselle Ramirez and Alicia Partnoy
November 23, 2016

A: Today is November 23, 2016. A thick booklet you have there. Oh my gosh, a bunch of stuff that you need to do for your surgery!

M: Well, this list here is the postoperative medications that I'm supposed to get. So I'm going back and forth trying to get my doctor to prescribe them.

A: What are they?

M: Pain meds? I don't know.

A: This is an antibiotic, Bactrim, and then Percocet is a big pain killer, and Flomax probably. . .

M: Who knows! Yesterday somebody called from Arizona to talk about this document: "This is the forty-seven-page guide to what you need to do. Everything is in here."

A: [*reading off a page from the booklet*] "Candidate?"

M: Well yes, who is eligible to have this done, basically. They sent this to me weeks ago, and then they called yesterday to give me highlights about it.

A: Have you read it?

M: Oh yes, a long time ago. It's really detailed.

A: "Strict bed rest." For how long?

M: It tells you all these things. Going to the hospital, the operating room, what it's going to be like in recovery. Guidelines for your hospital stay, before your surgery, the day of the surgery, one day after surgery.

A: You didn't answer my question, but knowing how hard it is for you to not move around . . . [*reads from the booklet again*] "Arnica."

M: Homeopathic. The stuff before the operation is actually pretty entertaining because it goes like hour by hour, it's funny. Starting now, eight weeks earlier.

A: [*reading*] "Stop smoking." "Letters of recommendation."

M: That was happening in October. So then it gets kind

of more regular: Three weeks before, two weeks before surgery, the day before. Bowel cleansing preparation the day before. And here's what you need to do that evening, stop eating or drinking at midnight.

A: When are you going to travel?

M: December 20, and the surgery is the twenty-second. And then the morning of the surgery I have to be there at 5 a.m. You're fasting until you're done.

A: So, did you do all the medical stuff that they were asking for?

M: Yes, eventually.

A: Who's going with you?

M: I have to work this out, because when I get there, there are two former students who are out in Arizona and they've agreed to be on the scene.

A: So, this is Scottsdale, Arizona.

M: Yes.

A: The recovery center is by the hospital too, right?

M: The buildings are close to each other. I've seen them both.

A: So, you will be transferred to this recovery center, upstairs. Is there a bed for someone else to stay there?

M: I don't know, it's been weeks since I read these details. I have to find out.

A: What's the reference to "packing being removed" on page twenty-seven?

M: The stuff down there that's keeping the space open, I guess.

A: Oh, dilation!

M: That's something I have to do.

A: Did they show you any drawings?

M: When I was there, they showed me some pictures.

A: What happens if you don't do this? It closes like when you don't put an earring in your earlobe hole?

M: If you don't keep it open, it'll start closing on itself, that's the problem. As long as you're diligent, things are fine.

A: You're gonna be diligent!

M: Of course, I'm not a wimp. I'm going to do this. It's like working out every day. With the dilation, they tell you to do it before you go to work, to do it at noon, when you get home at night before dinner, and then do it before bedtime.

A: And for how long?

M: Several weeks. I don't know how long it is actually. Each time for fifteen minutes, four times a day.

A: Look at how many aspirin medications exist!

M: Yes, mostly everything is bad for me to take. I mean, I don't take stuff like that. I can send this document to you since it's a PDF. So, you'll know day by day what I'm doing.

A: So the nurse went through the highlights over the phone yesterday?

M: Yes, she told me some things to keep in mind. She told me about the no aspirin, she said the only thing that's okay is Tylenol. But ibuprofen, Advil, Aleve, those are all bad. She reminded me to stop supplements, but since I don't take any, it's okay. To stop the progesterone two weeks before surgery, to take spironolactone, which is the anti-testosterone drug, up to the day before surgery. That's fine. But yes, it's just entertaining. She confirmed to me, "Your pre-op visit will be Wednesday, December 21 at 9 a.m. December 22, your surgery day, you need to be at the place at five in the morning."

A: So early, good that you'll be very close to the hospital!

M: Right! At midnight I stop taking liquids and solids. She said, "For your bowel prep, follow the detailed instructions on pages fourteen to fifteen." I went through a colonoscopy a few months ago. I remember that process. The other thing is that today I got a call from the Ear, Nose, and Throat department for Kaiser. See, last time I saw my Kaiser therapist, he said, "Remember they added coverage for voice training, and for having your Adam's apple removed." Then out of the blue, today I'm sitting here with a student, and ear, nose, and throat called. "Hi, we see we have a referral. We need to get a date, when can you come see us?" So I'll go December 13 at 2 p.m.

A: That is for the voice, or for the Adam's apple?

M: The Adam's apple, I'm guessing. I'm assuming that's why they called. We'll see. All that happened since you and I talked last time. Now I'm just trying to get my doctor to prescribe these drugs.

A: You don't need these drugs until post-op!

M: I just need to leave with them, apparently. She said that they don't have a Kaiser pharmacy out in Arizona. So that's why they want me to buy them now.

A: How do you get from the airport to the hospital?

M: They have a person who picks you up, who just emailed me yesterday.

A: That's for you and for your visitors?

M: No, visitors are taking shuttles or whatever.

A: So your kids are going!

M: I have to find out when.

A: Let's see what Santa brings you there. [*laughs*]

M: Yes, well, I'm gonna walk away with a different situation than when I walked in, which is fine. That will be an adventure! I'm more bothered by not working out for so many days in a row than by the physical pain. I work out seven days a week, so for like nine days I'm just there.

A: You're gonna work out your pain. [*laughs*]

M: Yes, I know, we'll see.

A: You need all your energy to fight that pain.

M: I suppose, we'll see.

A: But there might be stuff that you can do.

M: Well, I'm going to take my camera, since they want you to walk. Maybe I'll be so in pain that I won't eat much and it won't matter, but we'll see [*laughs*]. The problem now is just getting everything done before I go, since the final grades for my students are due.

A: What else do you need to do before you travel to Arizona in less than a month?

M: I had a Christmas tree last year in my place. I don't know if I'll put one up this year since I'll be gone for the whole time. So, I may just pass on getting a tree this year. I'll be posting on Facebook and checking emails. I'll take books and read. I'll be happy to be up and doing things when I get the chance.

A: So, you're going back to classes in January?

M: The ninth of January.

A: How many days did they tell you not to work?

M: I fly back January 1, which is Sunday. A week later classes start. I'm assuming I can walk around and teach. I'm not worried about that too much. It'll be what it's going to be—I'm not too worried. I want to start working out at the YMCA again and doing normal things, and we'll see when that happens.

A: That is the hardest part for you?

M: Yes! Because any time I don't exercise I start putting on weight. It's kind of the way my life is. I think I'll be happy when next summer comes. Months will have gone by, things will be healed, I'll be back to doing normal things.

What Is It Going to Be Like on the Other Side?

Martina Giselle Ramirez, December 14, 2016

My life for the past weeks has been all about grading, even on weekends. Grading on Friday night, grading on Saturday night, grading on Sunday from 5:00 a.m. until 8:00 a.m., with a break to go work out before coming back to my teaching duties.

Last Sunday, I got ahead of the game and managed to have a free evening to finally read *Principles of Transgender Medicine Surgery* by Rondi Ettner, Stan Monstrey, and Eli Coleman. The book is filled with amazing scientific information and details. I read the whole chapter on the surgery process itself, which includes diagrams and a discussion of the different styles of surgery developed. I learned about a variant created five years ago, and about the traditional, most frequently performed surgery. That chapter discussed some procedures so old that they have not been performed for a long time.

I also looked into the discussion of hormonal

treatments and read the chapter on mental and emotional well-being. I was fascinated by the research on sexual response—the ability to be orgasmic—before and after the surgery. It presented a series of studies of people who had male-to-female surgery and female-to-male surgery, all with the data. I learned that, medically, they actually had ways of measuring orgasmic response—that is, how quickly you come to orgasm. They found that female-to-male individuals tend to have greater orgasmic response after surgery, but that male-to-female individuals seem to have reduced orgasmic response. They said that male-to-female individuals were not bothered much by that, because it made a huge difference for them to know that their body was finally in line with their emotional way of thinking of themselves. That is, they were less bothered by the mechanics of performance.

The book also discussed the ways people's preferences for partners change after surgery. Researchers discovered that a percentage of male-to-female individuals who historically had been interested in women became interested in men after the surgery. So, I just went to bed that night thinking: "Oh my gosh, what am I going to do in terms of a dating preference?"

I also read a study in which twenty-eight people who'd had gender-confirming surgeries were interviewed about their newly developed interest in dating men. I didn't read the whole book, but here was everything you ever wanted to know in one place. It was amazing! I went to bed Sunday night just thinking about how it was going to be when I came back. What will I be thinking? How will it feel? I had heard about some of this from two people I know who transitioned to female. They had done their surgeries at the same place I will have mine. Both of them at some point were dating men and women because they needed to figure it out. Then, both—as far as I know—ended up with women. They told me that they had to date people to figure it out. So, Sunday night, when I finally went to sleep, I didn't dream. I just went to bed wondering: What is it going to be like on the other side?

Reading that book made me reflect on how, for me, it is fundamental to find a life partner who is kind and not full of themselves. I dream about finding somebody I can trust innately, who will not desert me when things get hard.

Beyond whether this person is male or female, my big goal going forward is to find somebody who I can tell will never bail on me, someone loyal both in their heart and soul. Partners can disagree, but at the end of the day, you have to know that they are in your corner for life. People are not perfect. They stumble and mess up, but if they are true to you, they apologize and try to get up and be better again. Finding somebody like that is the big challenge. I guess I will have to leave myself open to the idea, "Who is to say what packaging they will come in?" I must acknowledge, however, that I have trust issues with men. I have seen the way they can be, and I have not always liked what I have seen.

Please, World, Let Me Get This Done!

Martina Giselle Ramirez

Sent: Tuesday, December 13, 2016, 7:23 p.m.
To: Athena Ganchorre; Catherine Coverley; Alicia Partnoy

Dear Friends,

Hope this message finds you all well on this December evening. :)

As you know, my gender-confirming surgery (GCS) is coming up on Thurs., Dec. 22 (talk about a cool Xmas gift!), paid for thanks to my Kaiser health insurance coverage. :)

Since each of you has expressed an interest in coming by to support me in my journey for at least part of the time I will be at the hospital, I wanted to share what I know at this point about the logistics.

BUT FIRST—*I want to say how much it means to me that you would take time away from holiday festivities to come be with me at all, especially since I won't be able to be my normal, get-up-and-go-do-fun-stuff self while you are around . . . so I am in your debt. :)*

And so, to the details I know as of right now:

Air Travel—I will arrive on Tues., Dec. 20 and will fly back to LA on Sat., Dec. 31 or Sun., Jan. 1 (I will be discharged at 2 p.m. on Dec. 31). For about 2 weeks, I have been playing phone tag with the person in the Kaiser travel office who will set up my travel to and from LAX. I'll share arrival/departure info once I have it.

Hotel Lodging—Last week and today, I spoke with the Kaiser person who handles hotel arrangements and other matters. She says that anyone who is coming to be with me can stay in my hotel room for free on Tues., Dec. 21 & Wed., Dec. 22, the two days prior to surgery when I will be there, as well as for any of the many days after when I will be in the surgery recovery care center. And so, I will book a room with two beds and will arrange for guest key access. They indicated to me the nearby hotels which meet the $100/night criterion, based on the reimbursement forms they process, so I will follow up with the relevant hotels tomorrow.

And so, while I hope to have the final word on travel & lodging tomorrow (please world, let me get this done!), here is some info you might find of interest in the meantime:

The guide given to patients who are undergoing GCS (see attached = all the details you may be wondering about— and more!)

A map of the area, with surgery center and nearby hotels indicated

Details for local hotels, courtesy of the MDs who do the GCS procedures [not that you have to worry about booking rooms, but once I pick one of these, you can check its amenities (workout room? Etc.)]

Well then, I'll get back to you as soon as I know final details . . . in the meantime, an evening of exam grading awaits (it's finals week now!),

Martina :)

ow much body fat you have and where it is. But
rently it comes from your sides. So I'm going to
er to make it deeper.

take all these things very naturally. I don't think
's the attitude of anyone without your scientific
ground.

pose. There are some really nice articles online
describe what they do. Some of these, in fact,
color photos—and be prepared, it's graphic. But
eally kind of cool to see what the doctors are
ng to each other. I've spent my life in the science
d, so I always know that everything they do to
is based on data or evidence. I appreciate it when
tell you what they're going to do clearly, when
e's a whole paper trail of publications and proce-
s that have been evaluated, defended.

you found this fascinating book that provides
kind of information, right?

Principles of Transgender Medicine and Surgery.
only reason I found that book is because I went
ur school library to just look at their new arrivals
shelf. The amazing thing is that I didn't have to
est the library to purchase it!

clearly have some allies there, don't you think?

Getting Ready for the Big Surgery

* *

Martina Giselle Ramirez and Alicia Partnoy
December 14, 2016

A: Finals week 2016. Today is December 14, and I just
came to say goodbye because I'm leaving to see my
parents in [Washington,] DC, and you are going to
the hospital. Is that in twelve days?

M: In less than a week. Yesterday I went to see a Kaiser
doctor about doing a tracheal shave. You know they
have these weird medical microscopes that can look
down your throat. So, he inserted one that went down
through my nose, looked around inside and said,
"Yes, things look fine." He then made a referral to a
doctor in Kaiser who trains surgeons for this procedure, and that doctor is going to call me to schedule
it. It's supposed to be a pretty simple surgery; you can
get it done and leave on the same day. I was impressed.

A: Going back to your gender-confirming surgery in a

Getting Ready for the Big Surgery

Martina Giselle Ramirez and Alicia Partnoy
December 14, 2016

A: Finals week 2016. Today is December 14, and I just came to say goodbye because I'm leaving to see my parents in [Washington,] DC, and you are going to the hospital. Is that in twelve days?

M: In less than a week. Yesterday I went to see a Kaiser doctor about doing a tracheal shave. You know they have these weird medical microscopes that can look down your throat. So, he inserted one that went down through my nose, looked around inside and said, "Yes, things look fine." He then made a referral to a doctor in Kaiser who trains surgeons for this procedure, and that doctor is going to call me to schedule it. It's supposed to be a pretty simple surgery; you can get it done and leave on the same day. I was impressed.

A: Going back to your gender-confirming surgery in a

few days. You said that you feel it's difficult for people to go visit you during the holidays. You sound so apologetic in your emails to all of us. I mean, you're obviously grateful, but you don't assume that we want to be to be there for you.

M: I know that, but remember I spent a lot of years living with someone who was embarrassed to be seen with me.

A: It's hard to undo all that, but let me tell you that in my case I pretty much want to accompany you, not just because of our book project.

M: I'm really touched by that.

A: Tell me what your worries are, if you have any, about this surgery and the hospital stay.

M: I'm worried about being bored [*laughs*]. I'm worried about not working out every day. Those are the big things for me. For the surgery, they put you under anesthesia, right? So, when you come out it's like, "Okay it's done," but then it's painful. There were a lot of things I had to laugh at when I read that forty-two-page guide.

A: You had to laugh?

M: Because they have a list of things to bring before you come. Let me find the list oh my God! Supplies!

A: The maxipad.

M: I was laughing when I saw that one. How many
   decades have I pondered those, and now I actually
   need them! There's a lot of stuff in this document:
   douching instructions, details.

A: How do you see yourself after this?

M: When I went to the consult visit to Arizona in March
   with the doctor who's going to do my procedure, she
   was examining me down there, and at some point she
   said: "Well, so I could make your vagina four inches
   long, or I can make it six inches long." I asked her,
   "How do you make it longer?" "I use skin grafts,"
   she replied. "Which do you think you'd want? I don't
   need to know right now, you can tell me when you
   come in December."

A: You need to know in a week.

M: I've decided I want it to be deeper. Because clearly it
   accommodates a guy's—you know—better.

A: It will also accommodate transgender people.

M: It will do anything. You get maximum capability by
   being deeper.

A: Is it more painful?

M: No, she says where they take the skin from depends

on how much body fat you have and where it is. But apparently it comes from your sides. So I'm going to tell her to make it deeper.

A: You take all these things very naturally. I don't think that's the attitude of anyone without your scientific background.

M: I suppose. There are some really nice articles online that describe what they do. Some of these, in fact, have color photos—and be prepared, it's graphic. But it's really kind of cool to see what the doctors are saying to each other. I've spent my life in the science world, so I always know that everything they do to you is based on data or evidence. I appreciate it when they tell you what they're going to do clearly, when there's a whole paper trail of publications and procedures that have been evaluated, defended.

A: And you found this fascinating book that provides that kind of information, right?

M: Yes, *Principles of Transgender Medicine and Surgery*. The only reason I found that book is because I went to our school library to just look at their new arrivals bookshelf. The amazing thing is that I didn't have to request the library to purchase it!

A: We clearly have some allies there, don't you think?

On Regrets, Reincarnation, and Resilience

Martina Giselle Ramirez and Alicia Partnoy
July 28, 2017

A: Caitlyn Jenner in *The Secrets of my Life* quotes Laverne Cox: "The preoccupation with transition and surgery objectifies trans people. . . .The implication is, you are not the real thing unless you have had a gender confirmation surgery," (p. 280). How do you see our book dealing with the surgery and avoiding that objectification?

M: Society objectifies women in so many ways! I know that if I changed my dating profile to be available to guys, I would have no lack of men contacting me because many would see me as a novelty. I can picture them saying, "Whoa, this is cool!" even without thinking about me as a whole human being with feelings and beliefs. And that's just one example. Everybody wants to just lift the hood of the car and see the parts. For me, what's more fundamental is what's sitting here [*pointing to her heart*].

A: When I read Jenner's clever discussion of Laverne
    Cox's statement, I became concerned that our discus-
    sion of your surgery would be seen as another form of
    objectification. The thing is that I like medical stuff,
    and I'm curious about these processes. I also think
    you are so brave. Sometimes I find myself thinking
    that it's so easy for me to be a woman.

M: You came this way out of the box.

A: You have to go through all this pain.

M: I'm just trying to get the best deal I can, given my
    circumstances. This is why I think about reincar-
    nation in some religions. Would I love to be born
    as a woman in a cisgender woman's body? Yes, for
    sure! Because I could have my own babies. To have
    someone kicking around inside me, to nurse a baby.
    Those things I missed, and will never get to do.

    Back in the 1990s when I was working at Bucknell
    University, I was in the car with somebody, and they
    were telling me they just learned that they were preg-
    nant. We were on this long drive from some shopping
    mall, and I was mostly quiet on the way home because
    it hit me: No matter what modern technology can do,
    it can't make me a cisgender woman. I certainly have
    people who said, "Oh, this transition is all about you
    just wanting to wear pretty clothes. You just want to
    look nice." No, it's not that at all. That's like icing
    on the cake. The cake is way more fundamental.
    Would I love to come back in a different body? Abso-
    lutely, absolutely! As much as people talk about the

challenges of having monthly periods, and having your personality changed by that—

A: Well, that is not fun, and of course many women don't have any interest in having children, but at least they get to choose—at least these days, much of the time they get to choose. I mean, we have to fight for that right to choose, for those patriarchal governments and religious leaders of the world not to rule over our bodies as they wish to rule over yours.

M: Now I'm just escaping all the bad things the testosterone does to you, because really at this point, I'm just trying to repair the damage that it does to your body. My God, I wish I never had testosterone affecting me this way. Of course, I don't know if they had testosterone blocking technology back when I was a kid, and even if they did, I couldn't afford it. I get regretful sometimes, but I've never let a lack of money or people's negative attitude stop me. I've dealt my whole life with people just dissing me. "Are you sure you should be doing this PhD?" You just learn to do the best with what you have available, and that's what I did. That's why I never contemplated suicide regarding my gender dilemma.

A: Some people can't stop it. I don't know enough about mental health, but sometimes you are what they now call resilient.

M: Yes.

A: That resilience is what helps you bounce back.

M: That's why you can see my smile in those old photos! It's not fake, I'm not pretending. I was really happy, but I knew inside that I could be happier, or happy in a different way, if I had the choice to be authentically me. But my reality doesn't invalidate the life I had before, that's why I'm not ashamed of it. I don't need to lock it away to make sure nobody sees it.

My Contributions to Promoting Diversity

Martina Giselle Ramirez, March 12, 2017

"One high school student reflected this nation's almost touching faith in higher education when she said: 'I think my main concern is that without a college education I'll have slim chances in today's world. I want a better life for myself. That means college.'"

—Ernest Boyer, *College: The Undergraduate Experience in America*[20]

The above excerpt from Ernest Boyer's *College: The Undergraduate Experience in America* highlights the fact that college years are widely viewed as a vital stage of life. It is a period when a student's process of vocational discernment—what sociologist Julia Aaker and colleagues defined as "the path one follows to discover areas of interest and action that provide meaning in one's life"[21]—can potentially be resolved. Students acquire the background and skills needed to move forward in their post-college years, along their chosen path.

During my doctoral studies at the University of California, Santa Cruz, from 1981 to 1990 I was involved in teaching and mentoring programs for minority junior high and high school students. I did that through the university's Saturday Science Academy and by working in the Minority High School Student Research Apprentice Program. In the Academy, I conducted science demonstrations and field trips on Saturdays for students from the Pajaro Valley Unified School District and the Salinas Union High School District. In the summers of 1987 and 1988, via the Apprentice Program, I worked with five students from Watsonville and Salinas High Schools.

For ten weeks each summer, these students helped me with field work and genetic assays in the lab. That laboratory was the first iteration of what since then I have called the Spider Lab. In 1987, I worked with Pam Lum, a student from that first summer. Pam eventually got a PhD from Johns Hopkins University and is now a faculty member at the Community College of Southern Nevada. She recently came to Loyola Marymount University to drop off one of her daughters at a summer science camp, and we had some enjoyable time catching up on our lives.

From 1988 to 1991 I taught innovative sections of Introductory Biology to first-year minority students at the University of California, Santa Cruz. The course was an initiative that I had originated and developed for the Academic Excellence and Emerging Scholars programs. That class prepared students to grasp lecture material. It made them better scientists by helping them develop skills

Young Pam Lum and Martina in the research lab at UC Santa Cruz, July 1987.

Pam Lum and Martina at Loyola Marymount University in July 2016.

in critical thinking, public speaking, science writing, field and laboratory methods, and statistical data analysis. It also exposed them to the types of software packages used in the scientific process.

Later in my career, during my years as a faculty

member at four institutions during the 1990s (Pomona College, Bucknell University, Denison University, East Stroudsburg University), I continued to foster the success of women and underrepresented students. I welcomed them into the various iterations of the Spider Lab and provided mentorship to help them succeed in their academic endeavors.

At Pomona, in fall 1992, I cotaught a course with Laura Fandino for the college Freshman Seminar program entitled Minorities and Women in Science. Laura, a senior biology major and Spider Lab member, was later my coauthor on the paper that emerged from our work, which was published in the prestigious *Journal of Arachnology* in 1996.[22] She obtained her PhD at UC San Diego, and is now Director of Environment and Sustainability Programs at UC San Diego Extension.

I was able to keep supporting minority students at Bucknell through their Scholars program. There, I was a research mentor for Harrisburg-area minority high school youth in the summer of 1994, while they worked in the Spider Lab alongside college students conducting genetic assays. We all took a weekend sampling trip to Presque Isle State Park in Erie, Pennsylvania, where they helped map and then sample more than two hundred burrowing wolf spiders. One of my Bucknell students who helped me supervise and train the energetic young scientists was Wendy Farr. Wendy was a first-generation college student from a small town in northwest Pennsylvania where, she had told me, drinking, drugs, and sex were all too common among teens, leading to their limited success in life. Wendy later graduated from Ohio State University as a Doctor of Veterinary Medicine. She is now a veterinarian in Pennsylvania.

Since I "returned home" as a faculty member in fall 1999, I have had the greatest latitude to contribute to the diversification of STEM (science, technology, engineering, and math) at Loyola Marymount University. On campus, I became faculty advisor to the student chapter of Chicanos for Creative Medicine from 1999 to 2007. The Society for Advancement of Chicanos and Native Americans in Science chose me as their faculty advisor from 2008 to 2015. I also joined the Planning Committee for the California Forum for Diversity in Graduate Education in 2000. Much later, starting in 2015, I was able to again offer my Minorities and Women in Science course.

However, and without question, my greatest contribution to diversity during my years at this university has been the continuation of the Spider Lab. Aside from generating highly cited papers concerning genetic variation, reproduction, and heavy metal biomagnification in spiders, the Spider Lab has continued to be a superb training experience for its members, and one that provides a foundation for their future successes.

Over the years, the Spider Lab has been perceived as a welcoming and friendly space where considerable camaraderie exists and "cool" work gets done. Students working there have always been mostly female, with a significant number from underrepresented groups. In fact, the Spider Lab was exclusively female for seven years starting in 2003, until a single male joined in 2010. Many of these students have also been, like me, the first in their families to attend college.

While my research program has certainly led to a better understanding of many aspects of spider biology,[23] it has also contributed something of perhaps greater value to the institutions that have employed me and to the wider world—human capital in the form of the alumni of the Spider Lab. It also ensured that increasing numbers of professionals in STEM fields will be women and members of underrepresented groups.

Martina, Aira Wada, and Yuka McGrath in the Spider Lab, June 2018

Martina with Aira Wada, Jazmin Quezada, Yuka McGrath, and Angela Abarquez at the start of summer research, May 2018

Reunion at the Hospital

· ·

Martina Giselle Ramirez and Alicia Partnoy
December 29, 2016

A: Today is December 29, 2016, and we are recording our conversations again, this time in your hospital room, just seven days after your surgery. Do you want to talk a bit about how you feel? You've been posting on Facebook—

M: Because I wanted people to know that I was fine.

A: Have you been feeling emotional? Your daughters came to spend time with you, and you've spent some time by yourself reflecting on all these things.

M: Doing the kind of outings we did when they came to see me after surgery hardly happens in Los Angeles. Pretty much the only contact I have with the younger one is when I go to her performances, and part of that is because she's so busy at school as a double major.

So during the year she's under a lot of pressure. If she gets away, it's because she goes to visit relatives for the holidays, but because I'm not there anymore, I seldom get to see her. It was really neat to have them around again for a little bit, because I've had several Christmases by myself in recent years. They would go off and I would be taking care of the kitty cat.

A: I'm so moved by the fact that their mom drove them to visit you after surgery. I think that was very generous on her part. How are your daughters doing? What did you talk about?

M: The thing that was important for me, a big thing, happened last night when we were driving back from our dinner at Denny's. My older daughter and their mom were in the front seat and my younger daughter was in the back seat with me. At some point I asked, "So what would be the highlight of your two days here?" My younger daughter asked me, "What was yours?" And I said, "It's the fact that you came." I don't know if she recognizes how significant it is that I wasn't alone. I said, "The fact that you came to see me, it made the holidays less lonely." I think that touched her.

A: Tell me more about how you spent those days with them. I saw some pics on Facebook of you beaming, walking out of a secondhand store with a neat new outfit.

M: I was happy to be with the girls all day long! We went

to dinner both nights, and the waiters would be like, "So what do you ladies want for dinner?" Once upon a time, that would have been traumatic for my ex, to be around with that kind of thing happening. Everybody who looked at us seemed to think, "Here are some women out shopping for the holidays," and it wasn't a big deal.

Having them around for two days was pretty important. To have my former student Athena around was also important, in a different way. Now Catherine Coverley, another former student, wonders when she should come by tomorrow. You might want to interview her because I've known her since fall of 2004. She's at the University of Arizona Medical School, which is the same place where Athena is. One is a faculty member, the other a medical student.

A: We need to figure out a schedule for her to talk to me while you're busy with the dilation routine.

M: Right! Because, basically, that rules my life. Every couple of hours I have to come in and do this for about half an hour each time, and then I'm free.

Interview with Catherine Coverley: Lessons in Acceptance

Catherine Coverly and Alicia Partnoy
December 30, 2017

Catherine Coverley with Alicia and Martina in Scottsdale, Arizona, December 2016

A: Can you tell me how you met Dr. Ramirez?

C: I met her on my third day of college at Loyola Mary-mount University. It was the late summer of 2004, and I had come all the way from New York. I had never been to California. I had never even been on an airplane before. During my first few days on campus, I had a meeting with Dr. Ramirez and I felt so welcomed! She immediately started to discuss some research opportunities with me and connected me to academic resources. We began working together in the lab, and that started a collaboration that lasted all four years of my college experience.

A: Did she present as female when you were at Loyola Marymount University?

C: Never. Dr. Ramirez was a male. During my four years with Dr. Ramirez, he was constantly happy, smiling, laughing, and joking. He was very congenial, jovial, and gregarious, although he probably was more reserved around professors.

A: Why did you want to be here for her after her gender-confirming surgery?

C: The mentorship that developed on that very first day at Loyola Marymount, and the continuing support that I received from Dr. Ramirez over the past decade, has been overwhelming. The level of support that I received emotionally and academically from this one person changed the entirety of my university experience. I know that Dr. Ramirez's presence was a pivotal part of my college years.

A: Can you share an episode where her presence had a positive impact on your life?

C: During my second semester at Loyola Marymount University, my mother was diagnosed with end-stage breast cancer. Dr. Ramirez communicated with her by phone, and I filed papers to transfer out of the university and go back home to New York to help my mom. But she worked with Dr. Ramirez to create a plan that made sense for me and had my best interest at heart. They forged this creative plan to get me to stay in Los Angeles and still feel I was supporting my mother.

A: This is so moving!

C: And that's just the tip of the iceberg. Dr. Ramirez is also responsible for the opportunities I've had to present at conferences all over the country and all over the world at this point. My initial interest in research came from her. So there's no one I would rather support through something that's as difficult as her surgery. I'm trying to keep my emotions under control, but I'm also a first-generation college student, and it was very rough being at a school with such affluence. The wealth of the students at LMU was overwhelming for me. It was like nothing I had ever seen in my life.

A: Where are you from?

C: From Buffalo, New York.

A: Why did you want to come to Los Angeles?

C: It's every New Yorker's dream to make the westward trip and move to Southern California. Also, I'm Catholic, and Loyola Marymount is a Jesuit institution. I believe in its mission around social justice. I'm from a very low-income family, but I won a full scholarship to that school, so I went there.

A: And then Martina told me that you became class president at medical school. Is that right?

C: I've done so many things!

A: Do you remember the research you were doing with Martina as an undergraduate student?

C: I worked on every project that went through the Spider Lab—at that time we were doing research about population genetics and paternity in different species of spiders. I had my hands in many projects and helped in the lab in general. We would give tours for prospective students. I was seriously involved for a long time.

A: What is the most important lesson you learned from Martina?

C: It's difficult to answer because I learned so many lessons! But I would probably say that it's about acceptance. I was seventeen and fresh off the airplane, all alone because my parents had not been able to travel with me. I came into the glitzy, glamorous, affluent environment that is Loyola Marymount University. It was this extremely conservative institution with mostly all wealthy people—they were working to make it more diverse, but it wasn't there yet. Being accepted by Dr. Ramirez instantaneously, and him just having this unconditional love and inclusiveness, was so amazing. He was like, "I'm going to accept you and make you feel part of this family, part of this community. And I'm not only going to accept you and treat you very well, but I'm going to take you to places in your career and academics that you couldn't have gone to otherwise. And I have no qualms around that. You don't owe me anything. I'm just going to give to you and accept you."

Dr. Ramirez has faced so many struggles with acceptance, and when she felt she wasn't wholly herself unless she underwent this transition, there was fear that she wouldn't be accepted by this very conservative university. But the story of how that evolved, and how it actually was a supportive institution around her transition, and how many students from different backgrounds supported her, just says a lot about Dr. Ramirez. She received the level of acceptance and care that she has offered to me and so many other people.

A: Speaking of the support she received at school, had Dr. Ramirez transitioned back in 2004 or 2008 when you were still attending Loyola Marymount, do you think the climate would have been the same as today's?

C: I think that because Loyola Marymount is Catholic, it is an accepting and loving institution. I believe that if Dr. Ramirez had made the transition during my time there, between 2004 and 2008, she would have been accepted. What provides evidence to this is the fact that Dr. Ramirez wasn't sure if the Dean of the College of Science and Engineering would be accepting, back when she was initially transitioning. However, he instantly stood up in her support and made that support public. I think that says a lot about the university. The Jesuits and the professors there take acceptance and inclusion seriously.

A: Do you want to add anything?

C: This whole transition, and the bravery that came along with it, makes me very proud of Dr. Ramirez. The pushback, the animosity, and the hatred from the majority of the population toward people who undergo changes like this, is reason enough for most people to not be this brave. You're supportive, and Athena is supportive, and I'm supportive, but most of the country is not. Loyola Marymount is now an interesting institution, forward thinking, but not all are like that. I just want to reiterate that I'm very proud to even know someone like Dr. Ramirez, let alone to have her be such a close, lifelong mentor to me.

My Doctor Is Trans

Martina Giselle Ramirez, December 29, 2016

This morning my surgeon came to see me and we had this amazing conversation. She performed my gender-confirming surgery exactly one week ago, and she always makes me feel relaxed and in the best hands. I had initially contacted Dr. Toby Meltzer, the director of the surgery center in Scottsdale, Arizona, and I thought at first that he was going to do my gender-confirming surgery. However, the moment I met Dr. Ellie Zara Ley, I was happy to become her patient. She is professional, experienced, and has a warm and cheerful personality. This morning I was telling her about my feelings and thoughts, and she shared a bit of her experience, including the last thing that I had expected: My doctor is trans!

She told me that Dr. Meltzer had hired her not because she is transgender, but because she had the right personality, demeanor, and intentions to come into the field of gender surgery and into his practice. She said that many others had wanted to join him, and she felt fortunate to have been chosen. Her academic history is what really sealed it, being a plastic surgeon who had undergone full general surgery residency, followed by multiple specialty fellowships in plastic surgery, hand surgery, microsurgery, and craniofacial/pediatric plastic surgery! Plus, she said, Dr. Meltzer had gone down to Tucson to vet her by watching her perform pediatric surgery at one of the hospitals where she worked.

Dr. Ley had her gender-confirming surgery sixteen months before at this same hospital and on the same floor. She had been a male physician at four different hospitals, so her transition was very public—it had to be negotiated at these four places. But it was smooth because at each hospital, a human resources representative announced, "From now on, Dr. so-and-so will be known as Dr. Ellie Zara Ley, and she will be using the women's restroom." That was kind of astounding.

I also asked her about her relationship situation. She shared that she had met her wife in her junior year in college, and that they had been married for twenty-one years. They had not yet divorced, she said, but they were separated. However, they continue to be a family for their two teenage daughters, who live with their mother. Dr. Ley told me that they vacation together and spend nearly every weekend as a family. I wasn't surprised to learn that, as in my case, things between her and her wife are better, even though her wife still keeps a certain distance. I was moved to hear her say, "This big cloud of mixed emotions is over my former wife. I can't seem to clear this cloud, despite trying to love her as best as I can, as the 'new' me."

Then I brought up the book *Principles of Transgender*

Medicine and Surgery, which talks about these issues, and she hadn't seen it before. I mentioned some of the chapters that had made a big impression on me, like the one about the surgery, and the chapter focused on emotional and psychological issues.

I told Dr. Ley about another study in this book that looked at people's romantic interests and how they change after their gender-confirming surgery. For example, if your interest was initially in men, did that persist after you transitioned? And if your interest was initially in women, did that persist? What the researchers found is that sometimes people stay the same in terms of interest, and sometimes they change. When I mentioned that study, my doctor said that she still considers herself gay (lesbian), but even when she recognizes that a rare selection of men may still be attractive to her, she doesn't think that she could actually follow through and be with one in any capacity.

She still had not really put herself out there for dating, but she was open to it, although she wasn't sure anyone would put up with her heavy weekday work schedule, and her need to be away with her daughters every weekend. She felt lonely in Phoenix, and missed her family a lot—she missed her loving wife from the past, and she wished for her to come back, although she recognized that she had taken her husband away, turning her life upside down. "Transitioning had big consequences, both positive and negative," she said. "I'm happy to be free and to be me."

I wanted to talk to her more, but she had to go do a medical procedure. Really, I wasn't expecting this long and inspiring conversation with my doctor, and it was special to realize that both of us had been through the same experience in the same place.

Giving Birth to a New You: On Pain, Stuffed Animals, and Being Silly

Martina Giselle Ramirez and Alicia Partnoy
December 29, 2016

M: I was surprised that this process of recovering [from gender-confirming surgery] didn't mess me up more. I was really surprised because the vaginal dilations went okay, with the plexiglass dilator going all the way in. No problem. Fifteen minutes, I just watched the clock. I didn't get bored. It was really easy. And the fact that a week after my surgery I'm walking around for an hour and a half!

A: I thought I was going to wheel you home, but it's more likely that you're going to wheel me home!

M: I was just as surprised!

A: In terms of the people you had around, do you wish you had told someone else to come visit?

M: No, I was really so thankful to anybody who came. It's Christmas and New Year's, and everybody that I know is very busy. The only time off they get is for the holidays, so if they managed to get away to see me here, it was a big thing for me. I certainly didn't expect anybody to be able to do that.

A: So, Christmas was the day that you felt worst because nobody was here to visit. I see the balloons—some friends prepared you for that lonely day.

M: Had I been able to walk around, it wouldn't have been so bad. The first days after surgery they let you walk, but you can't leave the building. If I had been out on my own with nature, with my camera on Christmas Day or Christmas Eve, I would have been fine. But the fact that I had time on my hands and I couldn't go outside was difficult. Also, it was really hard for several days to do basic things like tie my shoes, lean over—or if I dropped something it was like, "How am I going to get that?" It was just so tight, with the stuff that was in there. So once all that came out, things very quickly got a lot easier to do.

A: What do they scientifically call "the stuff they left there?"

M: What they do when they create the vaginal space is put in packing material. They showed it to me when they pulled it out. It's gauze. It's a big pile! I was amazed. I was like, "Wow. All that was in there?" Once that came out it was such a relief! Then the doctor cut

away several stitches and pulled them out. Within a
day or so, it became much easier to move around.

A: And was this the first surgery ever for you? You had
never been under general anesthesia, right?

M: The only serious thing I had before was a colonoscopy.
And as a kid, we were too poor to have health care. I
had stiches in my hand when I was little, and I had to
go to the ER, but that was it. Things people take for
granted, like dental care, we didn't have access to, but
I was a really happy kid despite all that. I just learned
to make the best of what I had. Yard sales and places
like the Goodwill store were a big deal for me because
you can get stuff for not much. I was resourceful—
I got parts and I built things. I've built bikes out of
parts.

A: Did you ever have stuffed animals?

M: Only when I was very little. I've seen them in pictures,
but I don't really remember them.

A: Tell me about Aya, that stuffed creature who has been
with you these days. You take her places, and you
take pictures together.

M: I guess one of the things that I envied about women
was that they had a lot more freedom to have fun
and to just be silly. And I was raised by a dad who
was conservative, Catholic, Republican, and also ex-
military. He was intimidating. There was never any

space for me to be silly. But just going through life, I noticed that the women around me had stuffed animals when they were tiny babies, but also when they were older, and if you went to their homes, you noticed their stuffed animals on the couch, for example. Nobody feels weird vibes about that, and I thought that was nice. Then, when I got my own place with a loft bed, I was like, "Wait, it's kind of lonely up here. There should be little critters waiting for me when I climb up at the end of the day." Now there will be.

A: Did you talk to Aya when there was nobody here? You just told her goodbye when we left the room for dinner.

M: Sometimes.

A: Is it somehow therapeutic for you, like for some people talking to their pets?

M: What is true about pets is that they love you unconditionally. Your dog, your cat, they don't care what kind of day you had, they love you. For me, finding a human being as generous as that in my life is something I would like. Finding a human person with those qualities would be really awesome. Still, I'm basically a very happy person. There's not a lot that gets me down.

A: Somebody wrote on your Facebook page that you are, in a way, giving birth to yourself. I thought about that pain you had to endure as the pain of giving birth to a new you. Do you remember who wrote that?

M: Oh, I don't remember, there are so many comments!

A: Cassandra was her name.

M: Oh, yes, I know her! She transitioned several years ago.

Reflections after My Gender-Confirming Surgery

Martina Giselle Ramirez, December 29, 2016

I always remind people that for every person who is able to have gender-confirming surgery, many more lack the means to do it. The only reason I could have this surgery was that my insurance covered it. Therefore, I feel fortunate, while I continue to be well aware of and concerned about others without these resources. For example, a recent cost estimate just for a male-to-female gender-confirming surgery was near $100,000, an amount I couldn't have afforded without a supportive health care provider.

For most of my life I did not have such resources either. During graduate school, for example, I had to send money to my parents to help them survive financially. If you are from a wealthy background, you have no concept of these realities. Logically, I knew I didn't have money to afford my transition. In a way, that's why I got married: I wanted to have kids, and I thought that, because of my poverty, transitioning and raising my own children was never going to be possible. That's why I got married, not because I wanted to be a male. I just wanted to have a family, and I realized I could not have it the way I wanted. Had the circumstances allowed it back then, I would have made different choices.

I have been public and open about my transition, even when I could be totally private about it. There are those who want to be in the public eye because of their big egos. For me, it's really a question of helping make the world more accepting of people on this gender journey, making their lives easier, so they do not become a casualty.

I think the more individuals who personally know someone who is on this journey, the better. For example, if you ask most people at our university if they know someone who is transgender, you will probably get an extremely short list, if any list at all. If you ask about awareness, they might mention Caitlyn Jenner and some other media personalities. However, in terms of people they know in real life, for many I am the only one.

Historically, people in academia only felt comfortable nurturing affluent white men. They did not want women, they did not want the poor, they did not want anybody who was not the "norm." Therefore, once I became successful in academia, I tried to help others who experienced discrimination. I felt that if I was public about my transition, I could help effect change in academia's hiring practices and demonstrate the value of having an inclusive faculty for the sake of the students. Today, university administrations believe it is valuable to have faculty role models from different ethnicities, genders, and class backgrounds. I believe students should also see those who are trans in leadership roles in higher education.

I believe that the more people get to know someone like me, the less influenced they will be by the talking heads online, or by the conservative talk show hosts who call us evil and perceive us as God's abomination. If you don't know anybody personally who is transgender, it is not necessarily hard to get taken in by those irrational voices. That's why I am open about this to the extent that I am. My life has been focused on helping people, and that is true with regard to my gender transition as well.

Leaving the Hospital: A New Year, A New Body

Martina Giselle Ramirez and Alicia Partnoy
December 31, 2016

Martina at the Arizona Canal, during a walk around Scottsdale, Arizona a week after her gender-confirming surgery, December 2016

A: Today is December 31, 2016, and we are about to leave the hospital. How do you feel?

M: Well, very different than when I got here! [*laughter*] It's going to be a story of managing my body and figuring it out again. See, for years my life has run on schedule: getting up in the morning, working out, coming to meetings at 8:15 or 9:00 a.m. Everything was finely tuned. So this whole situation is now totally different, because I don't know how often I have to pee and when. I got up last night several times. Is this is going to become normal? I have a loft bed at home, so going to pee means climbing down the ladder, which is fine, but it'll be nice to be able to predict how many times I'll have to do so. Besides, I never know how quickly pee is going to come out—if I get an inkling something might happen I head to the restroom. The other thing is figuring out how much physical activity I can handle. Walking around for an hour and a half nonstop was pretty good. There are instructions about what kind of physical activity you can do. But I have a hunch I'm probably ahead of the curve compared to many people.

A: Do you feel uncomfortable with your body?

M: No, but I guess we're going to see. I'm not really bothered by what's going on down there—I can clearly see the healing areas. The nurse showed me this morning the sutures that are dissolving on their own, which is really cool, since I can feel these sort of "ridgie" hard things down there now. She says eventually they'll just go away on their own, peeling off and falling off, which is cool.

But it is so different going to the restroom. Each time I wonder, "Okay, it's going to come out in some direction," but I have no idea. It doesn't seem right now that it's all coming out the same direction. I asked the nurse about that this morning, and she said, "Well, until everything heals and the swelling goes down, you're really not going to know what the lay of the land is down there." And they have me on stool softeners, which is fine I guess, but at some point I'd like to know if I could just stop taking them and see what happens. They're concerned that I'll have difficult bowel movements, which is not good for the stitches back there. So we'll see what I do when I get home, and I'll look at the instructions and follow them to some extent, I suppose.

As for doing dilations, that's been no problem going in all the way. It's been pretty easy.

A: But it's a new routine.

M: Yes, I'm going to have to figure out the bodily functions.

A: Tell me about this room. You spent several days here. What do you like the most about it?

M: I love the view—the fact that whether it's raining or sunny, these trees outside have flowers and I often see birds going to them. When I was sitting here some days, if I got the sun coming in at sunset it got too hot, but if I waited a little bit until it went down, I often got these beautiful sunset lights on the clouds. Pretty dramatic.

A: What do you like the least?

M: The bed. It works for some people, but it doesn't work for me. Hour by hour on my back. Last night was better than most nights, because they took the catheter out so I didn't have this pipe—

A: Coming out of your belly—

M: So, I tried sleeping on my belly for a while, then I tried on my side. That was pretty nice, I didn't really get too messed up last night. But the surprising thing was waking up at six o'clock in the morning and all of a sudden, within an hour and a half, I went to pee six times!

A: What would you have done differently when planning for your surgery and your stay here?

M: Oh, it's funny because they wanted me to bring all my medicines, but at the end of the day they supplied me with all I needed. They told me to bring tampons, but then they had a giant pile of tampons. I own a whole bunch of embarrassing underwear and panties, which I use for working out. Because I grew up poor I use things until they fall apart, but I didn't want to bring those with me. So I went to buy a whole set of new panties. I also have a whole set of new pants, since they said you need loose fitting pants, and I bought five of those. But the reality is that most of the time, I was running around in a hospital gown. They have these disposable panties, plus they are giving you panty liners and other things. So I brought all this stuff for no reason.

A: What were the most useful words you heard from the nurse or the doctor here?

M: What clearly had the biggest impact on me here was a conversation with my doctor, where I found out that she also had transitioned and she had her surgery at this same hospital. I was quite impressed that she was willing to be so open. Other helpful words came from a nurse who came to check on me every day. She told me, "The problems you're having with pee? Other women have this issue too. Even cisgender women have this problem." That was good to know.

The Happiness Balance Sheet

Martina Giselle Ramirez
January 7, 2017

It's Saturday morning in my apartment in Culver City, California. It's been over two weeks since my gender-confirming surgery, and almost a week since I've been back in LA. When I returned to campus last week, many people asked me how I felt now that the big surgery was behind me. My standard reply was that I was very happy that it was over, and also surprised that the recovery process was quite easy for me (presumably a benefit of being in shape, thanks to working out every day).

On a deeper level, though, there is much more to being "very happy" than meets the eye. In fact, for me, happiness in this case is based on a mix of credits (good things) and debits (not-such-good things), which are associated with the surgery and other matters. And, as in the financial world, not all credits and debits have the same value. In any case, this mix of "balance sheet" items is as follows:

1. Credit: Being Liberated from the Impact of Testosterone. While I know that my male "hardware" is what allowed my two daughters to come to be, I was so relieved to find it not there after December 22. On a basic level, it was way easier after that to wear everything from a swimsuit to yoga pants (I no longer had to hide certain things). But on a deeper level, since that old hardware wreaked havoc in my life, with everything from my changed voice to facial hair to hair reduction in later years, thanks to the testosterone, I felt like I had been released from prison after being wrongly incarcerated.

Those who are not trans have no idea what it's like to be marooned in a body you know is not right for you but you cannot escape from. And all the while, you can see others around you who possess the sort of body you want, ones that change through time in ways you want (e.g., during adolescence). Like Moses in the Bible, you can see the Promised Land, but can never get there. Thus, having the testosterone source and the related hardware removed from my body represented a big psychic victory for me, and led me to being more at peace.

2. Credit: Finally Having a Vaginal Region. While it took many days until the post-surgery packing material could be removed, and while self-dissolving sutures are still in place along its sides, it's amazing to know a vagina is downstairs! Moreover, since I have to do vaginal dilations several times a day, I can check on its appearance and healing progress with a mirror. Once I've healed from the follow-up labiaplasty procedure this coming July, I'll have a much better sense of what its post-surgery layout will be like. In any case, if opportunities to become intimate come my way, I'll go into such situations feeling good about myself—and with the hope of feeling sexual pleasure in a manner that I've always wanted.

3. Credit: Having a More Feminine Body and Mind. More than two years of hormone replacement therapy has given me a body with great skin, breasts, softer edges, and fat deposits in new places. Indeed, I've gone from the scrawny distance runner I was when I came out in 2010, to the curvier Latina I am today. I also have a greater emotional range than I ever did, and I think of matters a bit differently, as I touched on elsewhere in this book.

Of course, like the former inmate I am, I also live with the legacy of what my years in the "male jail" did to me, which brings me to some debits.

1. Debit: The Things I Missed. There are so many things I never experienced, given my body as it was and the status I was assigned as a result. Two big ones are missing out on puberty, girl style (including the chance to have a moon ceremony, a traditional coming-of-age gathering that is common in many cultures across the Americas) and never having been able to carry and birth a child, and then be a mom.

2. Debit: Physical Features Impacted by Testosterone. While there are a multitude of physical legacies of the handiwork of testosterone, they are not all wiped away by gender-confirming surgery procedures. For example, when I get out of the shower every day, I see a face that, while happy, has less hair on top than back in my 20s. Seeing women on a daily basis on TV and at work who were not similarly impacted drives home what I lost along the way and was helpless to prevent. And while I have a voice that, to me, is expressive and lively, it's also in a lower range than it should have been—which is why I have to focus when on the phone so as not to be called "sir" and "Mr."

Medical avenues to permanently address such hormonal "damage" are not available to many, are quite expensive, and can have mixed outcomes among individuals.

Overall then, my happiness balance sheet postsurgery favors the credits, not simply because there are more of them, but also because I think their worth is *priceless*! Nonetheless, far from being all wine and roses, my life going forward will involve coping with those debits.

Quick Recovery and Ready for Chondrolaryngoplasty

. . . .

Martina Giselle Ramirez and Alicia Partnoy
May 26, 2017

A: Okay Martina, here we are about four-and-a-half months after your surgery. You got up at what time?

M: Quarter to six, I slept through my alarm.

A: I can't believe our lives are so crazy! This semester we haven't seen each other since your surgery. You're already bored of me, don't keep yawning! [*laughs*]

M: [*laughing*] This means I'm relaxing.

A: You are pretty recovered from your last surgery. That scar in your neck is really healing. The scarves look great on you, by the way. But I forgot the name of that surgery.

M: Chondrolaryngoplasty. Some people call it tracheal shave, because it removes the Adam's apple.

A: Oh, right. Tell me about your life after your first surgery. I was so shocked to see you returning to work immediately.

M: I didn't have much time, because the school year started on January 9 and I got back into town on New Year's Eve.

A: You taught an amazing number of students this semester.

M: Yes, I taught two classes with a total of eighty-two people.

A: And wasn't the doctor's recommendation to take it easy for the following two months after surgery?

M: That's what you're supposed to do, but then there's your job. So I didn't have much choice. I survived spring semester. My goal was just to get through the semester. I didn't do anything except my job. I went out to take pictures just twice in all those months. Pretty much every night I was at home grading. I would usually fall asleep at my desk and I would wake up after an hour or two, and that was such a regular cycle! I was sleeping less than four hours a night most of the time. I taught three times a week and did everything else for my administrator job. The whole mix was just bad.

A: No social life!

M: No. What did I do that was beyond the norm? Shop for food periodically, go to Ralph's, and then go home.

A: But you managed to schedule this chondrolaryngo-plasty. How was that?

M: I had it scheduled for the Tuesday of finals week. I checked in the morning of May 2 at 7:00 a.m. and I was discharged at noon. And then I was back here in my office that afternoon to prepare an exam that I had to give the next morning at eight. That week was strange because I couldn't talk very well, swallowing was a challenge, and sleeping was a challenge because there was tightness. My throat was swollen up and bruised. I had to sleep on pillows so my head was raised. The first few days were bad—they prescribed me pain medicine which made me constipated. They gave me, like, ten painkiller pills, but I took exactly one and said, "No more!"

A: You must have been in pain, but you sent nice greetings on Facebook to everybody who had supported you.

M: That was on those couple of rainy days. I thought, "If I'm out there and I'm cold and I'm wet and I can't talk, it is going to be so bad! So I stayed inside, kept warm, and graded student work. But the week after my surgery I was on a panel that featured three people who had transitioned under Kaiser's [Kaiser Permanente's] care.

A: That is wonderful!

Sharing Experiences with Mental Health Providers

Martina Giselle Ramirez, May 26, 2017

K aiser Permanente organizes trainings for their mental health providers, and they invited me to speak at a session focused on health care for transgender patients. The program featured Kaiser staff, who shared details of the coverage they provide, and a panel with three people who have gone through the transition via Kaiser's benefits. It was organized like a talk show, with an audience of about seventy people. The panelists received questions written on little note cards, and we sorted through them to answer those we chose.

One of the most interesting questions was, "Do you dream differently?" I didn't have time to answer that one but, in fact, when I first got on hormones, I remember having dreams in a different manner, more vivid and involved, cinematic. They also happened more often, as if a theater was in full operation.

I did respond to the question, "How has your transition been in terms of acceptance at a Jesuit Catholic

University?" I told them that I was surprised at the positive response. For eleven years, I had not transitioned there even though I knew very well who I was, because I was worried about the possible lack of acceptance. After I came out in summer 2010, I was curious about what kinds of comments I would have in my teaching evaluations that fall, but I didn't really see anything bad there.

That first summer, my dean visited my office one day to convey his support. I told the audience at the Kaiser panel all about the "bathroom blues" in our science building, and about that award I had received for student faculty research. The dean didn't have to support me for that prize, but he did, and I received it during an evening awards dinner. I hadn't changed my name yet, but I was presenting as female, with a dress and make-up. For me, this was a big sign of support because the school has trustees and donors who might be bothered by the fact that I'm trans. I mentioned this to highlight the choices made by people at Loyola Marymount University. They could have chosen to ignore what I was doing and avoid putting me in public settings. However, not too long after my transition, I was hired as Director of Undergraduate Research, and later, I became Special Assistant to the Provost. And just this summer, I was named Director of the Center for Teaching Excellence.

At the same time, there is a group of conservative alums and faculty at our school who think that the institution's Catholicity is going downhill. They call themselves "Renew LMU," and they are not happy when the university hires people who espouse views that don't fit with their ideas. LMU's leadership is aware of them because they cause problems periodically, but despite the potential to annoy this group by placing me in leadership positions, the school has supported me. It would not be hard for the Renew people to find out about my transition, but for some reason, they have not acted on it.

A Question of Community

Martina Giselle Ramirez and Alicia Partnoy
August 3, 2017

A: Did most of your colleagues at school approach you to ask how you were feeling after surgery?

M: Not really, just a few.

A: Is that because they're afraid of asking? This was obviously a serious surgery, and in these cases, generally your colleagues ask how you are feeling. Is it better for you that they haven't?

M: No. Well, keep in mind, this to me is a question of community or lack thereof. I wasn't really surprised.

A: But they knew you were going to have your surgery.

M: I don't think so. Of course I don't expect them to go and share details about their lives, either. But the people that are important to me knew what I was doing—and after I came back, they said, "Okay, how was it?"

A: So, most of the support, the concern, came from the former students?

M: Absolutely!

A: Again, I'm so sorry I wasn't that much in touch with you during these months! Life has been so hectic. But it was great to hear that you had a forum at that panel organized by your healthcare provider. You told me they have many transgender patients in southern California.

M: Back in March one of their nurses told me they were managing 1,300 cases.

A: Amazing! And is it both for male-to-female and female-to-male?

M: Yes.

A: When do you become "a case"? When you start the process, or when you go for actual surgery?

M: Once you begin taking advantage of their services, they start a case file for you where they record when you started hormones, and when you did any of these surgeries. [Kaiser Permanente's] transgender care services has a giant database of all the people that are going through their process. Because these are benefits, they're managing which ones they pay.

Interview with Selene Perez—Part 2: Martina Is Centered Now

Selene Perez and Alicia Partnoy
August 23, 2017

A: You have recently seen Professor Ramirez again, and you had time to catch up. How do you compare the Martina before her transition with Martina now?

S: Compared to when we last spoke before, I guess when she was in Pomona . . . ?

A: That's a lot of years!

S: I have to double-check with her—around sixteen to eighteen years, where we lost contact.

A: But it makes a lot of sense because it pained you to see her hiding her true self. When she started working at Loyola Marymount in 1999 is when she went more in the closet than ever before.

S: Oh, I didn't know!

A: Because it was a tenure-track job. But it makes so much sense with what you've told me, that you kind of cut the relationship because she had to block her real identity, she wasn't presenting as a woman, she had to hide.

S: But before, when I was living in San Francisco, she came over and I had a wig; it was like a reddish wig. I put that on her. I did her makeup and she dressed up. And we went out for the day, and I'll never forget. We were in a *taquería* in Santa Cruz, and she was dressed this way, and we walked in and people were looking at her, and some guy said something to her, and not in a friendly way, about how she was dressing. I asked him, "What is your problem? You know, we don't need that negativity. It's not like we're bothering you. Why are you feeling so upset?" That's what I don't understand. Why feel so threatened about people who transition? They are not hurting you, they are not sexually abusing anyone, or murdering people. I don't understand when people push their ideas or their insecurities on others for whatever reason.

A: They need to protect those so called "values" that they feel are at stake.

S: Well then, they are pushing their values on you.

A: That's true! Can we go back to this new encounter

with her after her transition? Did you see a change, besides the external appearance?

S: The easiest way of saying it is that she's centered. You can just tell she's a lot happier. Centered. Because if you are anxiety ridden, or not happy, you're not really centered. And a lot of the outside world can affect you.

A: So now you feel you don't need to distance yourself from her. Now you feel you can reassume this connection, see each other?

S: Oh yeah! She emailed me and she said, "I did my transition." I'm so happy for her, that she is finally able to live her authentic life. I was worried that she would get older and live like that, hidden. I couldn't even imagine, all of those years having to live like that.

A: To transition later in life seems to be harder, too. All that we learn living as women since childhood, you have to learn on your own. We have these conversations, and sometimes I tell her, "You sound like a teenager to me." I know she tells you about her love life, her desires, things cis women typically discuss in our teenage years.

S: She doesn't have anyone else to talk to. She's going through this alone. I tell her, "I can only tell you my experience. You're better off finding someone else who's also gone through the transition to answer those sorts of questions for you."

A: At the hospital, they were good at explaining medical issues after her surgery. I was there when they were giving her the instructions before discharge, and the nurse was explaining everything to her in front of me. I said, "Should I go out?" And the nurse replied, "No, you can be here." She was explaining all these things about UTIs [urinary tract infections]. I learned that she'll have to worry more about UTIs now than cis women do.

S: You bring up a good point. I'm a biology major, so none of that bothers me. It's all biology. I don't understand why society has this restriction on talking about certain things.

A: I told her, since she asked, "How do I know when I have to pee?" I said, "You just grab a bathroom. Whenever you see a bathroom, you go pee." Especially now that I'm sixty-two. Whenever I see a bathroom, I go. And I told her, "You might have to follow the same recipe."

S: That's a good question. There are things that she's going to have to learn, that we learn growing up.

A: It seems that Martina learned some lessons from you, even back then, when you were a teenager and you were advising her very cleverly. What is the most important lesson you have learned from Martina?

S: She taught me how to be a scientist. Really. All of that she taught me, since the beginning, when she was teaching me as a TA [teaching assistant] in UC Santa Cruz. I credit her.

A: This is important, a very strong statement. And she says you are happy with your career, right? You are at a good place in your career?

S: Yes, I am. I've been in biotech since 1995. Now I'm doing consulting work and I really enjoy it.

A: When you said she taught you how to be a scientist, what are the most important things that you need to know to be a scientist?

S: Critical thinking, data analysis, and writing, scientific writing. In fact, that's what I'm doing now, technical writing. The company I'm working for currently has a new drug, and whenever you have a new drug you have to write up an agreement—a legal document—for the FDA [Food and Drug Administration]. I'm writing certain sections of this document that they will be sending to the regulatory agencies for approval.

A: Usually people think, "Oh, I'm not a good writer. I'm going into the sciences because I will not have to write."

S: Even if you're a researcher, you still need to be a good writer to publish journal articles. I still use some books that she recommended back when I was a first-year student.

Interview with Morgan Mostrom:
On Solidarity

. . . .

Morgan Mostrom and Alicia Partnoy
May 16, 2018

A: Thank you for all your help while we are writing this book. I will miss you awfully now that you're graduating. Can you tell our readers about your contribution to this project?

MM: I was on the editing side of this process, making the interview transcripts a little less conversational and a little more formal. My main role was taking out "likes," or "buts," or "whatevers," or "ums" and piecing together sentences that trailed off to make them easier for readers to follow.

A: How do you feel now, when you are the one I'm recording?

MM: I am hyperaware! I'm thinking, "Oh, I just said 'like' and I just said 'um' twice, ugh."

A: That's funny! Morgan, can you tell me what has been the most fulfilling aspect of your work with us?

MM: To learn about Martina's story, the family in which she was raised, the community, the school, the backlash that she faced not only as a transgender woman, but as a woman of color, and a first-generation college student. It's been incredible to have firsthand knowledge of what she went through and her journey to where she is now, which is such a great place. Definitely the most fulfilling aspect was learning about her story, and how courageous she's being to share it. It's an honor to have been a witness to what you two are writing, and to be a part of the project.

A: Thank you! And what was the most difficult part of this job?

MM: It was hard when I couldn't quite understand what she was saying. I wanted to finish my editing and have everything fixed perfectly. There'd be, however, certain sentences I struggled with. I would ask myself, "Can I insert what I think she's trying to say or will that take away from the integrity of her story?"

A: Don't worry, that's our job this summer with Martina. We'll go over all your edits and make sure that everything comes across right.

MM: Perfect!

A: Has your awareness of the challenges confronted
      by people like Professor Ramirez been affected by
      your work on this book?

MM: I think it's definitely been affected. Fortunately, I
      had just read *She's Not There* by Jennifer Finney
      Boylan. It's a great book. You really feel taken
      into the story and into her mind and struggles.
      She, like Martina, is a college professor, so I did
      have the advantage of having just been exposed
      to that reality. But I think there's always more to
      learn about someone's personal experience and
      how they felt transitioning. For instance, reading
      Martina's accounts about dealing with the bath-
      rooms at colleges, I realized I had never thought
      about this additional struggle she faced. Not only
      is she dealing with all these pressures, but she has
      to deal with the fact that relationships change.
      I've gained more awareness of the struggles that
      people face, and also of the impact that women
      and men like Professor Ramirez have on other
      students. She was such a resource for students
      in the LGBTQ+ community at our university!
      I'm now more aware of the need for role models,
      people with whom students feel comfortable
      talking because they've been there. For me, to learn
      of the impact that transgender people can have on
      college campuses was awesome.

A: When I hired you to work in this project, the first

thing you did was to recommend *She's Not There*. Your generation has been more aware of trans narratives and lives, but maybe it hasn't read many books. What can you tell a fellow student who wants to know how *Happier as a Woman* can be compared to *She's Not There*?

MM: Finney Boylan's work had a lot of reflections too, but what sets apart Martina's narrative from hers is the fact that you are interviewing her. We not only get her voice, but also yours. And Dr. Ramirez gives great insight into her past and what it felt growing up; she also discusses her transition, the hardships that she faced, which were in *She's Not There* as well. However, Martina speaks to a very distinct point of view: The intersection of being a woman of color, a first-generation college student, and a transgender woman. These intersections really make her unique. I find it fascinating the way she talks about Christine Jorgensen. I never knew about her, and I think it's so cool to not only get that information, but to see how Martina's experiences connected with Christine's.

A: I was surprised that there was a very succinct reference to Jorgensen's narrative in Jennifer Finney Boylan's book. But then there were extensive references to other trans narratives, like James Morris's *Conundrum*. Finney Boylan writes beautifully, but at times I became a bit impatient with her book. . . . I thought she had the pressure to make it long. That's what scares me with our book. I need to deliver an amount of words that is huge for me as a poet. I'm reading other narratives and I'm thinking, "Ok, what are the risks of trying to deliver all these words when things can be said more succinctly?"

MM: Gotta find that arc. I have no advice for you there.

A: But you will give me some useful advice about the best ways to capture the attention of readers your age. You have all been exposed to trans narratives through the media, you have heard from the big personalities that Martina keeps mentioning, but what aspects of Martina's life and struggle should be given more emphasis if we were trying to capture the attention of younger people?

MM: When I think about our generation, I see that we get distracted easily, and we need something to pull us in, like the stories of discrimination, or how difficult they make the process to change your birth certificate. It's things like that that we don't know and that pull us in because we assume that if we know about Caitlyn Jenner or Laverne Cox, we know about transgender issues. But then you hear Martina say something like, "I had to get my original birth certificate from my mom, and then get a typewriter to fill in a form to change my gender there, and then mail it to Social Security." It's just crazy.

A: Now you can relate to this better because of the forms you had to fill in to teach in Spain after graduation, but also because the typewriter was so heavy for me and Martina to carry across campus from where she borrowed it, that we had to enlist your help to bring it back.

MM: Right! Really, I think that younger people will relate to any story about what Martina has to face on daily basis. I, personally, am always interested in the family relationships—

A: They are not here that much.

MM: I mean if she's comfortable talking about them. . . . A lot of us would want to know how her kids feel. That was for me the most interesting part of *She's Not There*—learning that you loved this person and you still want to be married to that person, but then you change, and how does that person feel? Looking at the complexities of relationships around the transition is what interests me.

A: And the images? What do you think about the photos?

MM: Photos are really helpful to see how Martina used to look as a child growing up compared to now, for example. I've read a few celebrity memoirs more targeted toward my generation. In Anna Kendrick's, for instance, she would be talking about a phase in her life and she would include the middle-school yearbook photo. I liked that, because I could picture her in the moment.

A: Morgan, this book project highlights the construc-
       tion of a discourse of solidarity, or the way we build
       solidarity with our interactions around Martina's
       life, her voice, her story. From all the conversations
       you have edited, which ones have more potential
       to reinforce this solidarity, this discourse of being
       supportive?

MM: I think what is really important is her relationship
       with her students, and to highlight the role that she
       has played in so many people's lives. The whole
       book is a discourse of solidarity because you're
       writing this to get her story out there. But it is also
       important to see moments of other people strug-
       gling, and her being in solidarity with them, and
       then hearing about how things have changed from
       Christine Jorgensen's to Martina's time.

A: I thought a lot about that and one of my problems
       with the other narratives is that when you need to
       quote from those books, you need permission, you
       need to pay to reprint their words.

MM: Oh, to use several of Christine Jorgensen's quotes
       you'll have to pay?

A: With hers I'm very lucky, the process will be a bit
       less complicated because the same company who
       published her book is issuing ours.

MM: That's so cool. What publisher is it?

A: Cleis Press. It's also the publisher of my book *The Little School*. Have you seen it?

MM: Your book? I just ordered it.

A: Oh no! I had a copy for you. I didn't dedicate it yet, because I thought: "Maybe she got it." [*laughs*]

MM: Well, I'll have two copies.

A: You'll have two copies. But coming back to Martina's book. What else would you like to see Martina and me discuss?

MM: I don't know what she's comfortable sharing, but from the actual transition process, the surgery . . .

A: I was there for both surgeries.

MM: I would find it so interesting to read about that!

A: I wanted to go with her to the first surgery, because if you've ever been with someone at a hospital, you soon learn that they need an advocate. My older daughter had three babies, and I tried to be there with her. The last time, she had a doula, and it was amazing, because doctors respect doulas much more than the mother of their patient.

MM: Right. You wanted to be an advocate for Martina.

A: So, I travel to this small town thinking, "Ok,

she needs an advocate, somebody who will be helpful." Guess what, I was wrong! Everybody in that hospital knew all they had to do to keep Martina comfortable as a patient, the attention was amazing.

MM: That's wonderful. I remember reading in *She's Not There* about hormones, and how that changed how she felt drastically, and that was really interesting too. And I remember Jenny would say in the book something like, "And all of a sudden, things that would roll off my back before started to make me cry all the time." And that stuck with me.

A: Well, sitting here in this office, we had all these interviews when Martina was in the first stages of her hormone treatment, and there, tears would come to her eyes so often, that I always had the Kleenex box handy. There are several recorded interviews where you can even hear sniffles.

MM: You have the amazing position of having known her before and after; you talk about how now she's a happy woman and how before you seldom saw her smile. Also, when I took a Women and Gender Studies class we learned about how difficult medical care can be—getting health insurance, getting doctors to treat you, and to acknowledge your new gender.

A: But the interesting thing is . . . I could be an advertisement for Kaiser Permanente.

MM: Because that's who she has?

A: Because they paid for all her surgeries, and not only that, they paid for her trip to Arizona to have the surgery.

MM: Oh, my gosh!

A: They paid for a room in a hotel so she could be there when checking out of the hospital. While she was in the hospital, her friends and family her support system, could stay in that room. I had the hotel room for free while she was in the hospital. Her daughters had been in the same room the day before I came their mother had driven them to see Martina after the surgery.

MM: That is remarkable! I'm floored!

A: The shocking thing is that when I tell some people about this amazing support from her healthcare provider, they would say things like, "What? This insurance pays for this, but my insurance doesn't pay for one more day in the hospital after surgery!"

Diet and Exercise Techniques for Voice Training

. . . .

Martina Giselle Ramirez and Alicia Partnoy
May 26, 2017

A: Our first recording was about voice training, remember? It was about this software to self-train, but now you found out that Kaiser [Permanente] provides voice training too.

M: I've only been to one session, and I have another one soon.

A: What are these sessions about?

M: If you record males and females, they speak in different ranges, women at a higher pitch, males at a lower pitch. The goal if you're male to female is to try to boost your range, to go higher. There's a zone of overlap between the low end of the female range and the high end of the male range. They want to boost you at least into that overlap zone. I got handouts about everything, from diet to exercises. Part of the business of modifying your eating habits is to avoid things that stress your vocal cords, like spicy food or cold drinks.

A: Oh, I thought you weren't drinking cold water because of the chondrolaryngoplasty!

M: No, it's for the voice training. I used to have my water bottle in the refrigerator all the time, now it's just at room temperature. They encourage you to consume warm drinks, but there are certain things that you need to avoid, like caffeine. What they're trying to do is to make your vocal cords better. So, I've tried to change my habits, and I don't drink cold drinks anymore.

A: Is that hard?

M: My standard drink is iced tea, so now when I go to any function, I guess I'm going to get herbal tea. They also encourage you to have throat lozenges, but only a certain brand because some of them have chemicals. Then they give you exercises to learn how to breathe from your diaphragm. When you watch babies breathe, did you notice that their bellies rise and fall? When you're a kid you normally just breathe from your diaphragm, but when you're older, you get used to breathing from your upper lung space. But if you really want to speak with the maximum capacity, you need to breathe from your diaphragm.

A: This is fascinating! Isn't it what all of us should be doing, not only to sound better but to live more relaxed lives?

M: Yes! Every night, I sit on the floor with a mirror, or I have a cup on my belly, and I work to make it rise and fall, rise and fall. They want you to do some vocal exercises, like say certain words or combinations of words and hold your finger to your nose so you can feel vibrations. All these are designed to help you project better. The therapist had me speak into a recording device and she said, "You have a lot of vocal fry."

A: What is that?

M: Vocal fry is a sound we produce when we talk because of low vibrations of our vocal cords. It shows in my recordings as static in the background. If you look at the recording, you can see something that looks like musical notes, but then there are all these dots in the background, and that stuff is "vocal fry." When I do these exercises I have the clearest voice. I can tell that when I'm on the floor and breathing from my diaphragm, I speak better.

A: So, this is going to be for about six weeks?

M: Multiple sessions. Who knows!

A: And your insurance pays for all these sessions!

M: Right.

A: Are you familiar with what other insurances are covering?

M: Not really. Kaiser is one of the first companies to provide coverage for transgender patients, but there must be others.

Our Children, Our Choices

· ·

Martina Giselle Ramirez and Alicia Partnoy
May 8, 2018

A: I asked Morgan—my research assistant who is helping us transcribe the interviews—what kinds of things would make this book interesting for her generation, which has been exposed to many trans narratives. Her answer was, "More things you go through every day." For example, she went on and on about the fact that you had to get a typewriter to change your name.

M: [*laughs*]

A: She found that fascinating, maybe because we asked her to bring that heavy typewriter across campus to return it to my department. Then she had to deal in a very tangible way with that machine. She wondered why they make you fill in the form to change your name on your birth certificate with a typewriter.

M: In the twenty-first century?

A: And most of her generation has never seen an actual typewriter. She also mentioned the surgery. I said, "Don't worry, we have interviews after the surgery, and piles of documents."

M: [*laughs*]

A: And then she said "family relations," which she had found enlightening in Jennifer Finney Boyland's *She's Not There*. Boyland stayed married after her transition, and her little kids were so accepting that they coined that word "Maddy"—from Mom and Daddy—to call her. I've been meaning to interview your daughters, but I don't know how they would feel about it, and I don't want to be like a vulture intruding in their lives.

M: Since my girls didn't choose to have their dad transition into womanhood, nor to have the family unit fall apart when I moved out on my own in 2015, I've chosen not to include their voices in this book. I know that those changes caused both of them great pain, something I'm quite sad about. At the same time, I think they now see that life on the other side of my transition is in some ways better than it was before. For example, their mom and I are more civil with each other, compared with the daily friction between us that was part of home life when we all lived together. And I know they realize that I'm different in good ways, compared with the dad they lived with, especially during those final years—less tense, happier, and more at peace.

A: Your daughters have been very supportive and, to a certain extent, their mom has too. Remember when she drove them all the way to visit you after your gender-confirming surgery? I thought that was amazing, but it shows that she was thinking about the well-being of the girls.

M: This is the mom whose prime directive in life was avoiding embarrassment.

A: Right!

M: For me, she was always concerned about what people were going to think. Me, the person she had married, changing genders in public, how much worse could that have been? That's where the whole business of not wanting to be seen with me came from. Similarly, her attitude has been to avoid embarrassment for the girls.

A: But they are adults now.

M: I know, I know. It's really up to them. I have regrets about the way life here in LA was organized for us as a family. The idea was that my life was just about working like crazy in that science building. Meanwhile, they're doing Girl Scouts and other adventures, and what was I doing? Just trying to make money to support the family by always teaching summer school.

And you realize you have no friends because you're working all the time, and you're not really seeing your kids.

A: The paradox there is that you were spending time nurturing the careers of so many students, and your own kids were missing you. That happened to me somewhat in Argentina. When I was twenty years old, I decided to risk my life for the future of my country, for its children, so my own daughter didn't have to grow up under a dictatorship. The paradox was that this decision ended up depriving my own daughter of her mother for three years. I know that the ones to blame were the military authorities who took both her father and myself to a secret detention camp and to prison for three years. Ruth lost contact with us, and she could've lost us forever. Your circumstances are very different, but sometimes we do things for our children that end up affecting them.

M: I wish I could have lived a life where I left work at five every day. I never had that. I wasn't home till later at night.

A: I know, my younger daughter—who was born while I was working on my PhD, teaching and lecturing here and there, and later on a tenure-track job—tells me she doesn't have memories of me from when she was a little girl.

M: I don't know, it's just not the way to do it. The fact that I was the only breadwinner for decades generated a lot of friction with my wife. It was like a bad soap opera, a bad drama.

A: Except that you had to endure that instead of watching it.

M: Yes, it was not just watching it, it was living it.

On Looks, and Trans and Cis Women

Martina Giselle Ramirez and Alicia Partnoy
July 28, 2017

A: In *Redefining Realness*, Janet Mock tells us that when she's getting ready to leave her doctor's office in Thailand, after her gender-confirming surgery, the surgeon thanks her for trusting him with this surgery to help her be happier. Mock writes, "I liked his acknowledgement that the surgery was finally making me happy, it was a necessary step toward greater contentment."[24] This resonates with what you say about yourself. Also, let me confess that I just learned the term "cis" from her book.

M: [*laughing*] I wish I could have been cis.

A: Janet's discussion of realness and passing, and the effect of looks on her transition, was enlightening. She was so beautiful, even before hormone therapy, that other transgender women always commented that things were easier for her because she could "pass." She uses the slang word "fish." Back then, in Hawaii, "fish" were the trans people who looked like women. Mock advocates for dismantling the notion that your life is easy if you can pass. She says that it implies that cis people are more legitimate or valuable. This, she writes, is just another strategy to police bodies.

M: I think there's a ranking out there among women, even cis women, and this is just the trans version. Since so many individuals around us are not trans, people just apply the same standard to us that they apply to cis women. If you look at TV ads or catalogs, do they usually show plus-size people? Of course not. Are they going to be anything but spotlessly made up? Of course not. They're always going to be perfect. Even if you are a cis woman, if you're not stunning, they're going to think that you're less valuable, not worthy to be seen.

A: I was shocked to read recent ads in Argentina that wanted to hire women for office jobs who were between eighteen and twenty-five years old with good looks. This type of ad was very common when I was growing up there, but I couldn't believe they existed today.

M: It's the same thing for women broadcasters here, for example. If they consider you too old, they don't want to give you air time anymore. They know that you've got more experience now, but you're not attractive enough to be in front of the camera. And that is done to cis women, so with trans women it's kind of the same. Who gets all the air play in the trans world? People who are stunning to look at, and had all the work done to look totally spectacular.

A: Janet Mock is very aware of this because this is happening to her and she thinks that she should fight against it. I admire her for that.

M: I keep these things in mind because I remember how I was treated long ago when I was over two hundred pounds, or when I had no money. For example, my first car was an old Chevy Nova, 1964, that I bought for $150. I then rebuilt the engine. When I drove that car to school, I sometimes got comments about my "ancient" car, as in, "Is that the best you can do?" I continue to be aware of who's dissing people just because they're not what's considered to be the standard. When I started presenting as female, before I had a wig, before I started hormones, I was treated differently than I am now. Is that right? I don't think so. But again, I saw it happen to cis women as well.

A: Take age, for example. I'm invisible now because of my age. If I have purple hair they look at me a bit more, so let me have purple hair. I don't want to be invisible! [*laughs*]

Getting Ready for Labiaplasty

Martina Giselle Ramirez and Alicia Partnoy
May 26, 2017

A: Have you received a thick booklet of instructions yet?

M: This time a nurse called and told me to write down this list; she sent me an email as well. It was basically, "Here are all the details you need to know before you go." It is pretty descriptive, but much less so than for the gender-confirming surgery.

A: And what is the name of this surgery?

M: This one is called a labiaplasty. And there is much less involved, which is good.

A: Still, you have to spend a couple of days in the hospital, right?

M: You're in the hospital one night and the next day

you're in a hotel. The morning of the third day you can check out and go home. The surgery is on Friday.

A: Since I don't have that fat booklet to read this time, could you tell me exactly what this is about? Do they have to take skin from your body?

M: What they do is create labia right around the vaginal space. They apparently do some shaping of that. But the other thing is, they put a hood on the clitoris.

A: With skin from that area?

M: Good question, I don't know where they take it from. But the thing is, right now there is no hood on the clitoris. They tell me that some people don't come back after the first surgery because they're fine with the way they are. But for me, I know that this is uncovered, because when I put pants on or do certain things, I realize that the clitoris is rubbing against that. [*laughs*]

A: Excitement twenty-four seven! Too much fun! [*laughs*]

M: I'm pretty used to it, but could we put a curtain over this thing? This is a little over the top [*laughs*]. So, I said yes, I will do the "part two" surgery. The other thing is that right now there are little remnants of sutures that are still down in that region. Most of them have come out, they have self-dissolved, but some of them I can still feel like little nubbins that are stuck. So they can pull those out. Also, the sutures on the side are pretty much healed up, but there's at least one that's buried. So, when I'm there they can take those out.

A: This time, my reason to go there is to see if I can interview your doctor, because last time she was super busy, and it was Christmastime. Last time, one of the reasons I wanted to accompany you, besides being a friend and wanting to be there, was because I know that when you go to a hospital you need an advocate. You need somebody who will help you relay your messages to the ever-busy medical personnel. I've been in hospitals with my daughter, who went through three deliveries with C-sections, I went with my parents multiple times, and I was in the hospital delivering my three babies, and I always saw the need for an advocate. The only exception was when my daughter hired a doula for her last delivery, but of course, she was a professional advocate. Last December in Arizona, it was the first time I was in a hospital where its personnel were always alert to the needs of the patient. I was there to keep you company and to help, but even if I hadn't been there, you still received all the attention you needed. Am I wrong?

M: All I had to do was press a button. And even if I didn't, they would just come in. I've never been in a hospital before, so it was all new to me. That was my first and only time.

A: After the labiaplasty surgery, when you come back home that weekend, do you have to teach on Monday?

M: Yes, Summer session two. That will be an adventure. Monday 4:00 to 7:00 p.m. I'm doing summer sessions one and two.

A: What are you teaching?

M: Genetics, a lower-division bio class, which I've taught in the summer for years. Getting summer session salaries will help me do things like buy another car, or a camera body of my own. The cameras that I use are owned by the university—they were purchased via research grants. So yes, I'm really looking forward to having some money. My twenty-six-year-old car is rusting out. I don't really like teaching the whole summer, but the upside is I'm going to have this money. I'm still paying two rents, given the situation that I have with my ex, so the more money I have, the better!

Interview with Athena Ganchorre—Part 2: Just the Packaging is Different

Athena Ganchorre and Alicia Partnoy
June 24, 2017

Athena Ganchorre with Martina and Alicia in Scottsdale, Arizona, June 2017

A: What is your job now, Athena?

AG: Basically, what I do is the same thing Martina did for me: I help students realize their potential. I oversee the academic services for medical students and I teach in medical school, but my primary job is to work with students so they reach their goals.

In medicine, there are exams that can open and close doors. If people want to go into surgery or into obstetrics, they need a certain score to even be considered. Medicine is driven by numbers!

A: What is your title?

AG: I'm the Director of the Office of Student Development at the University of Arizona, and I'm a research assistant professor in cellular molecular medicine. My PhD is in cellular molecular medicine, but they selected me for the position because I have a science education and a program development background on supporting students. Twenty years of my work has been mirrored after the program that Martina led at UC Santa Cruz and the ways she interacted with students. I've applied that experience, and later I learned the theory behind it. Also going to UC [University of California] Santa Cruz and taking feminism classes helped me understand Martina better, even as an undergraduate. We even had anti-war and feminist [activist] Angela Davis as a teacher!

A: Ah, I was going to ask you about Angela Davis. I've heard that she teaches my book about being disappeared in Argentina. But that's my ego kicking in. [*laughs*] She must have been an amazing teacher.

AG: She was. When she became a faculty member at UC Santa Cruz, there was a lot of political discourse around her returning to the UC's. Ronald Reagan, back when he was Governor Ronald Reagan, had told her in the 1970s, "You will never teach at the University of California." And many years later, she was back at the UCs.

It was really empowering to see her return to academia. Having a strong feminist program, with not only her, but also Asian-American faculty and LGBTQ+ faculty, opened my eyes. I was taking these courses alongside science classes. I don't know if it was just this marriage of things, but it gave me words, a language to understand what I was experiencing, and it also gave me a direction to lead the rest of my life. My sense of social justice will always be there.

A: I have this question that might or might not make sense to ask, because your experience has been so different from most people's experience with Martina. How would you compare the Martina before transitioning with her now?

AG: It makes sense! The best thing I can say is that I think our friendship, and the Martina I know now, is the same as before her transition. She is now able to be her authentic self, and I'm grateful that she could be. I'm grateful that I can witness that and I can be part of that journey. But she's not different, just the packaging is different, and that's absolutely important for her because now she feels legitimacy, she can completely be open and out. But she has always been the same person—that hasn't changed. In December, when I came to visit after her surgery,

I brought my partner and my ten-year-old son and both of them said, "She's a wonderful person." They didn't know her before. My son said, "She's really funny." And on occasion I got the pronouns wrong, and he told me, "Mama you say 'he' but she's a 'she,'" and I'm like, "Yes, that's right."

A: Oh, it happens to you too? It makes me feel so much better! My daughter corrects me too. My daughter, who was Martina's student while this transition was taking place, used to tell me, "You just said 'he.'" And I have a question for Martina about this, which I have not dared to ask yet, about how bothered she was when, while we were teaching together, and as she was already presenting as female, I sometimes would say "him" in front of my students. I know I just wanted to be swallowed by the earth. So, I guess you're answering me. I love the way you talk about packaging, because that's the way she feels. She says, "I'm the same person. Why doesn't Rose understand that I'm still the same person?"

AG: When she started openly wearing dresses to work, I remember we spoke on the phone because I was coming to Pasadena for a research project at the Jet Propulsion Laboratory. I said, "I want to come see you. Let's connect." We spoke on the phone for hours. We used to talk for hours, we still do. She may not remember that conversation, but I do because it was very symbolic for me. I remember I was sitting outside the student building. It was during my office hours, but I went outside to talk with her. That day

I told her, "I think I'm going to get a divorce." And in that same conversation she said, "I'm starting to openly wear dresses." And I said, "Looks like we're both going through changes." In my mind, it felt like we were both launching towards our true path, we were finding our voice, we were really starting to test the waters of how far we could go, of who we really can be. When I saw her in Pasadena, we went shopping, and we went to get makeup.

A: Was that before her tenure at my school?

AG: No, it was after she had been there for a while, about seven years ago.

A: See, in my case, I knew this very serious professor I couldn't understand. I would ask my colleague in the Latino Faculty Association, "What's wrong with Martin? Why isn't he connecting with us?" And then he transitioned and suddenly she's smiling. So, I saw that, but this is probably my view, my angle. Martina was elaborating on this elephant analogy the other day, where different blindfolded people were asked to describe the elephant they were touching. Each talked about their perspective. This was the "elephant" I knew back then. Now it's another elephant.

AG: How interesting!

A: My last question for you, Athena, is: since you were here in December for her first surgery, and now

you're here again, why did you want to be here today
for her?

AG: Just being able to witness her journey and to see that,
after all these years, she's able to be out and fully
herself, it blew me away. We first met in 1988, and
knowing how far and how long she kept her dream
alive, and that she was able to realize it—which is
what she's done for everybody—is really amazing
and powerful. I am just so happy that I could be
with her along the dream.

Waiting for Discharge, Discussing Our Book

Martina Giselle Ramirez and Alicia Partnoy
June 24, 2017

A: How are you feeling? Do you have energy to talk?

M: They are going to come in and pull out the catheter. They said, "Once it comes out you need to go pee because we need a sample. And then after that you're chill. Go take a shower, get dressed and ready to leave."

A: So discharge is at 11:00 a.m.?

M: Let's see.

A: Let's talk about the photographs in our book. I realize that in Caitlyn Jenner's book, they are in exactly the same place as in Jorgensen's, all together in the center of the book.

M: To me the most beautiful layout is when you have the pictures interspersed as the chapters go by.

A: Right? Because they are sort of telling a story.

M: Yes, they're part of the narrative.

A: True. I've seen narratives of Holocaust survivors and they have the pictures interspersed. That will make sense, so we have to figure out what pictures go where in our book.

A Facebook Post One Week after Surgery

Martina Giselle Ramirez
July 3, 2017

Martina during her road trip to San Diego, California, July 2017

Facebook
July 3, 2017

Road trip to San Diego, a day of Adventure & the Unexpected, 7/2/2017 ☺ During the 3 hr. drive down to SD to see a former student in a performance which was part of the Fringe Festival, I listened to country music via Pandora, singing along with the women & regularly tearing up during mushier tracks . . . while wondering if I'll ever find a life partner to sing along with on such drives. Then, since the overly long drive led to arriving late to the performance, with late admittance not being allowed (sigh . . .), I then headed north to Crest Canyon Preserve, Del Mar, a spider collecting site which was featured in spider papers co-authored w/students in 2009 & 2010. While hiking in flats was not simple, it was way cool seeing the preserve again & thinking back to how different life was back then. Finally, during the long drive back to LA, I got a flat tire in Seal Beach, and so sat along the 405 where I was first visited by a CHP officer, and eventually by a roadside service guy who got me on the road again (thank you!). And so, after 3 surgeries in the prior 6 months & a day to day existence that was all about task & crisis management vs. having a life, hope the rest of the summer & year is more balanced/less insane/filled with more joy ☺

Used to Balance the Books?

Martina Giselle Ramirez and Alicia Partnoy
May 18, 2018

A: It's already May again, and we haven't sat down to talk for about five months.

M: That's crazy.

A: It is crazy. Thanks for coming to my event with the students during exam week. We did see each other last week at graduation, and at another event, but we haven't had much time to catch up. Tell me about the new developments in your professional life.

M: Let's see. I continued to be on the job market, as I have been for the past two years, and I was one of four finalists for a dean job in Utah. I interviewed out there in March, but ultimately I didn't get the job. At the same time, I applied for several positions here on campus. I did not apply for this one, but I was also one of twenty-eight professors nominated for director of the Center for Teaching Excellence (CTE). I was then invited to apply, and later to interview, and I got that job offer! I'm set to start June 1 as director for the next three years.

A: I'm very excited, although I must confess that I would have preferred for them to offer you a vice provost or an associate provost job, because you can exercise more influence on the life of the university from there. You still can exercise quite a bit of influence as director for the Center for Teaching Excellence. You're a natural.

M: I'm a really a good fit for that job. I have connections all over campus. I'm really excited, even though it's not the job I applied for in the first place.

A: It's a lot of work too, because you're going to be teaching still, right?

M: One class a semester. The nice thing is that there'll be an associate director.

A: Oh, good!

M: Who I'll get to hire. Plus, there will be administrative support, so it's not just me doing all the work.

A: And you're great at managing people who work for you. So you'll have to provide direction, vision, leadership.

M: Right. Since I got this job, I've been contacted by many units at LMU [Loyola Marymount University]. I'm also having a meeting with the dean of your college and her associate deans, so everybody wants to get in on the action. And my ideal is, with that image of the cantina in *Star Wars* in mind, that you bring all these people into the party.

A: Wonderful analogy. You spoke a bit about the applications for other positions. It's hard to pinpoint, but do you suspect discrimination in any of these?

M: Good question, and of course, you never know. The thing that I noticed in the list of people just hired by the provost's office is that the heat the administration was getting from the Latino faculty, because they've never had a Latino or Latina in those high-level positions, seems to have yielded some results. They hired a Latina, and also your colleague José. So now they can say, "Hello! Check it off, we met your demands."

A: Barely, because only one of those is in the top twenty positions in the school. I see it as just a token. I didn't go to the lunch for Latino faculty with the university president because I had to travel due to my mom's health, but I didn't like that his letter said, "Let's have lunch when the dust settles." When the dust settles it's too late for anything.

M: Yes, they want to talk *after* the decisions are made.

A: And in my culture, you don't do business and lunch.

You socialize, maybe oil the wheels while you eat together. I know that in the US, lunch meetings happen all the time, but then they are called "working lunches," with an agenda, and hopefully some solid outcomes.

I'm so tired of this. I don't have any personal ambitions, but it's not fair. We are in California, can't they find Latinx candidates for goddess's sake?

M: I've made it to final interviews two years in a row, and I sometimes wonder, "Am I being used to balance the books?" Because they can say, "Oh, we brought a woman of color into our final slate of four," but in reality they have other people in mind to hire. Is that the only reason I'm being brought in? Maybe, but I don't know.

A: You can't tell. What type of letters did you receive from the places where you were a finalist? Just business letters saying in legalese something that reads like, "We're sorry?"

M: That's all you ever get, and around here I wonder if they are worried about blowback. They got some from the Renew LMU group when they hired your college dean because she's feminist. So, I wonder if they worry about getting blowback if they hire a trans woman for one of the upper echelon positions. I don't know, but it's their loss. Look, if they wanted my talents they had a chance. I think I have a lot to give to LMU, but if they don't want me in those high level positions, what can I do? They

had two chances, and they didn't go for it, so . . .
[*laughs*]

A: [*laughs*] Yeah, we laugh. We don't want to cry.

Dealing with Heartbreak

Martina Giselle Ramirez, July 3, 2018

I never thought of dating somebody who was also trans, but at some point I realized that in the same way that I relate to people who are also first generation college students, or low-income, I might relate to another transgender woman, like Peggy. I also always look for people with big hearts, and without arrogance, and Peggy—despite her forty-two-page long curriculum vitae that is getting longer as you read this—is not arrogant. She could have acted like those high-flying faculty members who are full of themselves. She is, however, humble. Everybody loves her because she's productive and has a very helpful personality.

There are many parallels in our lives as well. She's a year younger than I am, she has two kids, and she financially supports her family. Her wife, like mine, had not worked outside the house for a long time, and like me, Peggy carries that financial load. She told me that she had wanted to transition during graduate school, and instead, she met her wife almost as soon as she got there, and they fell in love. So, she left graduate school with a wife and a daughter, and that was not what she had in mind before.

There was a lot in her life that resembled my own, and I think she felt the same way. I got the sense that if we stayed together, if we got married, we were both going to continue supporting our exes.

I connected with Peggy in a way that I had never done with anybody else, and part of that was because I could use technology. When I dated a woman named Norma in 2015, I had a cellphone, but it was an old one. Now, I had a phone that let me send videos to Peggy. She would send me videos of her house, or walking her dogs, and I would take videos of walking around Loyola Marymount University.

When I visited Peggy in March, it was a pretty magical time. We had been together for four months. During that time, I had framed pictures of her in my office and at home. I would tell her picture that I loved her, which was true. However, I had never told Peggy that I loved her, in a text or in an email, so I wanted to tell her that in person. Unfortunately, somehow it never seemed like the right time to do that during my visit.

The last night that I was there, I got sick, and I was sitting on her couch, just holding her and crying. She thought I was crying because I was ill, but all my tears were because I sensed that this was going to be our last time together. One notable incident for me during that visit was the one night when we were intimate. In contrast to what I had read in lesbian romance novels, Peggy's time with me seemed to have been done out of duty and lacked much sense of excitement and romance.

Since this was my first sexual experience post-gender-confirming surgery, I came away feeling desolate rather than elated. I noticed the next day that she had the Valentine's Day card I had given her on her nightstand. With a feeling that the end was near for us, on the last night of our March visit, I took a picture of my words inside that card. I somehow felt that I was never going to see it again, and I wanted to remember what I had told her.

After I came back to Los Angeles, we kept the tradition of texting every day. Whoever got up first would text the other person. We kept doing that after my visit, but in her texts, the terms of endearment like "sweetie" and "honey" had disappeared. The Thursday after I got back, I asked her about that change in language. She replied that she had wanted to wait for the dust to settle, but that some time before I got to her house, her feelings about me had changed. She said she had tried to recapture the magic when I was there, but it wasn't the same.

I'd had some reservations about the future of our relationship, but I wasn't expecting this. Since she is such a busy woman, I had just wondered where a relationship would fit in her life. Could I imagine myself with someone who was so busy all the time? I wasn't sure, so I had told my friend and former student Selene Perez when I talked to her from the airport that I wondered if in a couple of months I was going to break it off. And of course, there were the logistics. At the end of the day, she had her job up in the Rockies and I have my job here in Los Angeles. I was, however, ready to apply for jobs close to her. Several days later, I was crushed to learn that Peggy didn't love me anymore. I remember thinking, "Well, I guess you won't have to do this break-up thing yourself."

The rest of that Thursday and Friday were just a big mess for me. I thought about how transition for her had been easier because male hormones had never affected her as much. She had gotten minimal facial hair, and she never had male pattern hair loss as she got older. She had told me that whenever she grew her hair long, even while she was presenting as male, if people looked at her from behind, they just thought she was a woman. After our relationship was over, I was sitting there feeling inadequate. I had no clue why she didn't love me anymore, but I had to wonder if she was making judgments about my transition outcome. Who knows! Once she told me she didn't love me, it really didn't matter. What was I going to do, try to get her to change her mind? No. I really didn't want to know what she was thinking.

After I learned about her feelings, I spent days crying. I was crying at work and going home and crying some more. Two days later, on Saturday morning, my coworker Jessica Lee and her husband took me out for brunch. They must have thought, "We've got to get you out of this pity pot." A week later I was scheduled for a job interview, so, after brunch, I spent the rest of the weekend in my office preparing the job talk and my presentation. I'm glad I had something else to focus on!

Despite all my pain, I had learned that I could have a long-distance relationship, and I could use technology to keep close. And even though it didn't work out, I learned how much this technology can actually enhance your ability to be in someone's life, and that will certainly help me in the future.

Recreating the *Star Wars* Cantina

Martina Giselle Ramirez, May 18, 2018

People have been asking me about my vision for the Center for Teaching Excellence. My standard response is, "Do you remember the original *Star Wars* from 1977? That scene at the bar with people from many different universes was like a crossroads of the world. For me, that is the way the Center should be." It should be the cross-roads for the university. Our schools and colleges always seem like different planets, and the Center should be where everybody comes together to share our experiences about teaching and learning, about being teacher-scholars, about new technological developments in our field.

Although I remind people about all the workshops I have organized over three years to help faculty develop online and hybrid classes, my real claim to fame at Loyola Marymount University is that I'm really good at bringing people together. I am sort of a diplomat, or a matchmaker. Those are some of the skills I will bring to the job.

I have a framed picture of Dwight Eisenhower in my office. When someone walks in and asks me why that photo is there, I explain that he was chosen as Supreme Allied Commander in Europe in World War II not because he was the most experienced general, but because he had outstanding people skills. He was expected to work with the British when many American generals considered themselves better than them. Eisenhower would also have to work with the French, and with a whole array of displaced armies. He was expected to be a diplomat and play nice with everybody. This is how I see my job in the Center.

As soon as I get into my office, I'm going to paint it a nice color, and I want to have a couch in there with a coffee table and cute coasters. I want the whole Center to be a very social, welcoming place. Any time you are in the area, please come in, because there is a storeroom in the back, and there will often be leftover food from events in the refrigerator.

Feeling Like the Biblical Job

Martina Giselle Ramirez and Alicia Partnoy
May 18, 2018

A: Martina, how did you spend the anniversary of your surgery back in December?

M: The anniversary of my surgery? Well. . .

A: Did you celebrate it in any way? What did you do?

M: Nothing. The problem is that my eye condition started around the same time. I went hiking on Christmas Day in the afternoon, and by the next morning, my eyes were acting weird. I went to urgent care and I got an immediate referral to an ophthalmologist the next Tuesday. That was the first of four ophthalmology visits thus far in 2018.

A: Four visits and the problem is still there?

M: They also referred me to a neurologist. I had an MRI on May 7, and the followup appointment is a week from today to talk about the results. But in the meantime, I just spent five months basically dealing with this on my own. Focus is never perfect, my left eye isn't focused all the time, while my right eye is always in pain to some extent. The only break I get is when I go to sleep.

A: And the MRI is for both eyes?

M: Plus the brain region.

A: But they haven't seen cataracts or anything wrong inside the eyes?

M: No, they haven't seen anything. Why is there sensitivity to light in both eyes? Why is there always pain in the right eye? It feels like there's sand in the eye. That's why I sleep more these days, just to get a break. I cry once a day, at least, not just about this, but for me, 2018 feels like the story of Job in the Bible. I started the year in a relationship, and then it ended. I had this work opportunity and it didn't come through, and this eye thing appeared out of nowhere and has made my life totally miserable.

A: Why do you say Job?

M: If you think about Job, the character in the Bible, he has many tribulations—

A: And then he confronts God and asks, "Why me?" Right?

M: Yes. I read that when I was a kid, and I had forgotten what the point was, what lesson there was for Job to take away. I now think that it is probably to be patient and to trust that God does what needs to be done.

A: You are resilient, but this has been too much to endure this year.

M: Well, it's certainly a lot! On top of all that, I got rear-ended driving my car home yesterday.

A: Your twenty-six-year-old car?

M: Yes.

A: Oh, so that might help if the insurance gives you some money to buy a newer one.

M: Well, it didn't matter. I just told the driver, "Look, I'm shopping for a car, this thing is twenty-some years old." It doesn't matter, right?

A: You were too nice! My daughter went through a lot for rear-ending somebody and so you could have gotten money for the new car.

M: Well, do I really want to deal with that right now? No.

A: I know, your mental health is more important.

M: Pretty much. It would be another thing to deal with right now.

A: Yes. All these things! You're sitting there and then they just bump into you. But some good stuff happened too.

M: Obviously I got this nice job at the CTE, and there's been an outpouring of love for me, by loads and loads of people. There are people praying for me! One of my students, she is Jewish and her family remembers me at their Seder on Fridays. It's been really amazing, the fact that they think of me.

A: It's because you've always been thinking about others, and supporting others.

M: Somebody said to me, "Maybe this is supposed to be your chance to let others take care of you." I guess that is true. But it's scary, because it's hard to read now. Even to read emails is painful. How can I have a career if I can't do normal things?

A: Well, but, you can be trained.

M: I know.

A: Wouldn't it be crazy? You would fill in another spot? [*both laugh*]

M: Yes, I know!

A: Why did you think of that too? Why do we think like that?

M: Going through life collecting these attributes that make me be part of yet another minority . . .

A: You'll become more interesting to be hired by some employers . . .

M: I know, I know.

A: I'm sorry, I have to resort to bad humor!

M: No, no. That has occurred to me too. It's like, how many other conditions can I add to the list before I die? What else can I collect? But what really worries me is: how do you date someone if just going out and doing basic things is a difficult chore? Just going into any room is an adventure because you don't know what the lighting is going to be like. I wonder about that sometimes.

A: I know.

M: I mean, I'm hoping there are people with big hearts out there.

A: There are, yeah, even some men.

On Being a Happy Woman

Martina Giselle Ramirez and Alicia Partnoy
May 18, 2018

Martina at the Wrigley Memorial on Santa Catalina Island, July 2018

A: I was thinking that our initial book title, *A Very Happy Woman*, is so contradictory! I saw your postings on Facebook in January—you were planning a trip, you were meeting former students for lunch, and you were really happy. I remember thinking, "Now, here is Martina as a very happy woman." And that was the fitting ending to our book. But already your eyes were giving you so much pain.

M: Keep in mind, I was fighting against the default, which would be that I would never leave my office, and I would never leave my apartment. I don't want to be sitting in a dark prison. So I will force myself to do the things I used to do in the past.

A: And your relationship, too. At the time, you were visiting Peggy. You were happy.

M: Yes, yes, that's right.

A: And then the breakup happened. You will have other relationships, you're mourning now. But, do you think we should change the title to *Happier as a Woman*, for example? [*both laugh*] Because you *are* happier than before.

M: I am, yes, yes, yes. We can negotiate on the title.

A: But I was thinking, because all these things are happening like bad karma, it's a contradiction.

M: Think of your life, for example.

A: Yeah, ok! [*laughs*] Thank you, thank you!

M: I have not had a period like you did, being kidnapped by the army, tortured, and kept in that place where your friends were taken out to be killed, not knowing where your daughter was . . . all those things you write about in *The Little School.*

A: I know.

M: In those times you had no guarantee that you would ever see beyond that period, right?

A: Right! That's why I'm optimistic and always tell you that you can get through this.

M: In other words, I remind myself of what you went through, your three years in prison, and then to be forced to leave your country, your family, all that you loved. . . .

A: I feel good that my story helps you in some way, Martina.

M: Because I'm only in month five, right? And that's nowhere near what you had to endure. And I think of Nelson Mandela, twenty-seven years in prison and look, he had a whole wonderful life afterwards.

A: That's true.

M: So I have to keep my faith.

A: And yes, you are happier than before the transition.

M: Oh, absolutely!

No Regrets

Alejandra Loperena Molina, October 15, 2018

After Morgan Mostrom graduated, Professor Partnoy hired me as her research assistant to continue the work Morgan had started. Because both authors care about the opinions of their students, and I am an English major pursuing a career in creative writing and journalism, they asked me to write about my experience.

I went into this project knowing very little about transgender issues. The opportunity to work on this book, however, has turned into a special and rewarding experience. While I was transcribing interviews and working on the edits, I got to read a little of Martina's story. I was mesmerized by her narratives and the strength she showed while sharing them.

After reading about Martina's experiences, I have created a picture of who she is, and I'm hoping that the readers of this book may get to know her through her words as well. Professor Ramirez is first and foremost an educator, and she has taught me a lot throughout this experience, even about things that are not related to her transition. I appreciated the scientific information behind the surgery, and the crazy things that were required of her during her transition period, but that was not what I really learned from her.

I learned about love, gratitude, and perseverance. This book is not a play-by-play of the transition process, nor a before and after picture. This book is about the insights that she has shared about her life and the way she has shaped herself into the woman she is today. Her hopes and dreams, her quest for love, and her refusal to back down on the issues that she cares about are incredibly inspiring. One of the most amazing things I saw throughout this process is that she fights tooth and nail to define herself and how she wants to be regarded, especially in her professional life. She has no regrets, and actively seeks happiness in all aspects of her life, and I find that incredibly admirable.

One often forgets that being human, regardless of gender, is complicated. We juggle so many things, things that often become the very fabric of our identity. Some of these things present hurdles in life that can be difficult to get over, and hearing about people like Martina steadily working through those hurdles gives hope to people who may be trying to get through as well. It's encouraging to hear about someone who juggles so much and still manages to retain sanity. Martina has been juggling multiple aspects of her identity her whole life: her race, her socioeconomic status, her physical appearance, her profession, her social life, a marriage, parenthood, and being transgender. These do not define who she is, but they are an important part of her and her story, a story that is worth sharing.

People have been telling stories since the beginning of time. When people share their stories, they are providing windows into their lives, their personalities, their identities. It is so important that we share stories, especially those that inspire conversation about topics that are widely regarded as taboo. Members of the LGBTQ+ community have stood long enough in the shadows, afraid to share their stories for fear of what people would throw through that window they opened into their soul. It is time for this silence to end, and there is power in the words and teachings that another person can offer. No matter how different, everybody has a story worth sharing, and Martina found hers when she decided to match her outside appearance to how she felt on the inside.

I hope that this story inspires people as this process has inspired me to be appreciative of other people's experiences and my own privileges. I have learned much about the process of writing, of editing, but also about the importance that a particular story can have on the lives of others.

On Skin and Beauty

Martina Giselle Ramirez and Alicia Partnoy
May 18, 2018

A: Are you wearing makeup? Your skin looks beautiful. It's glowing!

M: I just put on coconut oil. I've done that for five years every night before I go to bed.

A: I have to try it! My friend Rebeca keeps giving me lotions for my hands, those treatment packages with gloves and all that stuff. I should be applying some lotion. My husband just washes himself up in creams, but I don't have that kind of patience.

M: Well, I had that skin condition, which started up in July 2017. It went away around February. It was a nightmare, and 2018 has been a rollercoaster ride too.

A: Yes, 2018 has been tough.

M: But let me tell you something fun that happened to me last week. I was walking by the Ballona Creek Channel, wearing the usual hat I wear to avoid the sun. There was a guy walking his dog. He complimented me on my hat and asked me where I had bought it. He thought my jacket was chill too because it has that spider logo on it. He said, "Oh my gosh, you look very pretty as well." He was like sixty-something, but that's not the first time that's happened, and people say this about my skin. Men and women just come up in meetings to ask me, "Okay, makeup or no makeup?"

Our Future as Healers

Martina Giselle Ramirez and Alicia Partnoy
May 18, 2018

A: Thinking about retirement. You too?

M: Yes, me too.

A: But you have a few more years to go.

M: I know. The question is: how many more years do I want to do this job?

A: When I was a teenager, I wanted to be a medical doctor, and afterwards, study to be a psychologist. But I fell in love and I did not want to leave Carlos to study medicine in Buenos Aires. Now I see my future after retirement as a healer.

M: Did I tell you that I'm doing homeopathy?

A: Oh, nice. Is it helping?

M: Yes. My doctor is wonderful. She is a lesbian and I first saw her for my eye condition, just before visiting Peggy. We have these two-hour appointments.

A: I spent many years as a kid doing homeopathy, taking all these little sugary things, and getting a bunch of vaccines for my allergies. It was truly helpful, but why two-hour appointments? My appointments were five to ten minutes long. What happens in your appointments?

M: She wants to know about everything. I'm recording dreams for her, for example, so I have a tape recorder up in my loft bed. If I wake up in the midst of a dream, I grab the recorder, press the button, and I just go.

A: Does Kaiser Permanente cover her services too?

M: No, I pay for the visits. I wanted to try this because I remember how homeopathy had helped Rose get rid of her asthma. Regular medicine never controlled her asthma, but homeopathy did.

A: These days I'm learning a lot about alternative medicine. I'm reading *Manifesto for a New Medicine*, a book that James Gordon wrote in the 1990s. I know Gordon because he was the doctor for two of my best friends in [Washington,] DC. He directs the Center for Mind-Body Medicine. He used to chair the White House Commission on Complementary and Alternative Medicine Policy. He is a psychiatrist, trained in both Western and Chinese medicine. I'm hoping to take workshops at his center when I retire. I'll learn more about alternative medicine, and maybe I'll even plant medicinal herbs in my backyard. I always wanted to be a doctor, a real doctor, not just a PhD.

M: [*laughs*] Well, I wanted to be a therapist.

A: You can still do that, right?

M: I know, I just have to figure out which letters I want, PhD, MA, MSW, LCSW, because there are a bunch of career options.

A: For you it's going to be easier, with your strong science foundations. I will not have the energy to take all the science classes, but Dr. Gordon is training educators and community leaders to help marginalized communities deal better with their health.

M: That's so great!

A: He and his team go to Palestine, for example, to train people there as paramedics, and in holistic approaches, which in those war zones are necessary. That's what I see myself doing in three years, but let's see what happens.

M: Sounds exciting.

A: But now this book is about both of us? No Way. It is about you. Let me stop my "Me, me, me," thing.

Surviving Dark Times

Martina Giselle Ramirez and Alicia Partnoy
July 13, 2018

A: Last weekend I was at the hospital with my mother after her surgery, and the nurse would ask her about her pain. She wanted a number on a scale from one to ten. Going back to your own numbers, your "happiness index," let's say that in March you were at a nine despite your eye problems, because you were going to visit [your girlfriend] Peggy and living this magic. After the breakup, let me guess, did you maybe go down to three?

M: Less than five, that's for sure. I mean, really dark times.

A: Awful times.

M: Keep in mind that for some weeks I would just study people's hairlines. At the YMCA for example—I was just looking at people who walked in, and just felt envy.

A: If this is a major thing, there might be some solution in the world.

M: I don't know. The point is, I generally don't do that anymore. But back then I would look at pictures of Peggy and tell [my friend] Selene about Peggy's beautiful smile. Selene would reply that I have a much nicer-looking face. The idea was, "Look, some people have one thing and other people have another thing." Why bother getting involved in comparing people?

A: I notice women do that a lot. When I was in prison in Argentina, I just could never understand why, while we were, for instance, taking a shower in those gym-like bathrooms without doors or curtains, my prison-mates would look at each other's tits and say, "Oh, yours are bigger than mine." I just thought, "Who the hell cares?" I was never concerned about those things, but it's kind of a normal behavior in women, I believe.

M: And the reality is that it's not healthy for your spirit.

A: It's not, but I don't know, many of these things might be driven by our instincts—our animal side might be at work there. And maybe I was made this other way, in which I didn't care to look at our bodies. "Just take the fucking shower and let me do my thing. I don't want to look at you." But I don't know if it's a gender thing—it might not even be a gender thing. Ok, but let's go back to those numbers: will you tell me today what's your number in our happiness index?

M: Well, it's higher. It's above a five.

A: Not much above a five?

M: The problem is that the eye pain is unpredictable, and the blurriness in my left eye is there all the time. Going through the day, the only question is how bad it's going to hurt. Some days I walk in here and these lights are annoying. Other days they're okay, but it's the same room, the same lights.

A: And the tests don't show anything wrong, like cataracts, macular degeneration?

M: No, my doctors don't know what it is. I've been to seven doctor's appointments this year. I also had an MRI, but the results were fine.

A: What kind of doctors did you see?

M: Two neurologists, and the rest were ophthalmologists.

A: When we publish our book, maybe the right doctor will come knocking at your door. It might even be a matter of body and mind, don't you think?

M: Whatever, if someone can take the pain away, I am ready, please show me. Kaiser does out-of-network referrals, and it would be nice to get one for the Stein

Eye Institute at UCLA. At some point before the end of summer, I'm probably going to my general practice doctor, and I'll tell her, "Look, no one knows what's going on, how long do I have to do this before you guys think about referring me out?"

A: That's great, Martina, but "at some point" when? Why not tomorrow?

M: Well, I'll be at Loyola Chicago next week, Tuesday through Friday.

A: Oh, ok. What are you doing there?

M: The Association of Jesuit Colleges and Universities has something called the Ignatian Colleagues Program. Remember that I was invited to be part of this spiritual journey, this eighteen-month-long program? The first event is a four-day orientation out in the country, fifty miles from Chicago.

A: Right! But this one is not the silent retreat . . . ?

M: No, you have group reflections and social events. Otherwise, it's like a conference.

A: Oh, nice.

M: So, I'm really looking forward to being out there. Part of my journey these days includes nurturing my religious beliefs. I started going to church the past three Sundays.

A: Do you find calm—solace—there?

M: It gives me a place to reflect in community. I think
    I'm a pretty exemplary person in terms of taking the
    Jesuit mission and making it real.

A: That's true.

M: I don't exist for any other purpose in life than to help
    people. And it's been that way since I was small. At
    LMU [Loyola Marymount University] we are always
    reminded of its mission: to be men and women for
    others, which is what I do every day. So, for me it was
    very odd not being in the church for so long. Jesus
    isn't around to help people, he works through those
    of us who are here.

A: This also goes back to your childhood education. I was
    rereading our first talks, when you told me that you
    went to church every day as a child. Then I freaked
    out. "Every day!?"

M: Well, back then it was because my parents were into
    that, and I had to accompany them.

A: But you always found inspiration in Jesus's life, his
    taking risks for a better world . . .

M: For some students, those who have been marginal-
    ized, for example, they see in me how they can follow
    their dreams. They tell me they are inspired when
    they see someone who gave up much along the way

to be her true self. I could've played it safe, I could've continued to tolerate the way things were.

A: But you were also very unhappy.

M: I was, but they see people around them—even in their own families—who put up with bad situations just because they fear that life would get more difficult if they changed.

A: There are risks, tremendous risks.

M: But the fact that I did all that, and came out alright on the other side, means a lot for many young people here.

Empowered to Go Back to Church

Martina Giselle Ramirez, July 13, 2018

A nother thing that has been part of my journey these past few months is spirituality. I find myself drawn back to the Catholic Church. It all began back in late April when I had lunch with Sarah Eiman, a former student who had graduated in 2007, and who is now a veterinarian. She told me that she was reading *Building Bridges* by James Martin, a Jesuit priest. His book focuses on the LGBTQ+ community and the Catholic Church and elaborates on the question of how the two can learn from each other. Father Martin argues that the Church leadership and its LGBTQ+ members can find ways to get along better.

Since his book came out in 2017, Father Martin has been invited to be a commencement speaker at several Jesuit schools, though sometimes people on the far right have pushed back at such invitations. Intrigued by my former student's comments, I got James Martin's book. I read it on the plane, on my way to visit my friend Selene in the Bay Area in May, and I was crying. I read it on the way back and I was crying some more. Every time I read his words, I cry. I think it's because I believe in the messages found in the Gospels and in the words of Jesus. So when I read the works of James Martin or other religious writers, I am always deeply moved by their insights concerning how to live a life in accord with the main message of the Gospel, which is to love your neighbor. Now I am working my way through his fourth book, and would like to invite him perhaps to speak at the Center for Teaching Excellence.

These past weeks, I also returned to the Church. I attend Mass on Sundays at the chapel at Loyola Marymount University, and plan to go to St. Monica's Catholic Church, which is listed as an LGBTQ+-friendly place. Katherine Montejano, another of my former students, got married there. She told me that for twenty-five years, that church has had a gay-lesbian group called GLO, and I learned more about it from their website. Katherine told me that she and her fiancé went through wedding counseling there, and she learned that a friend who is gay received marriage counseling from the same priest. The priest just told them, "Well, because of the Catholic Church's position on marriage, I can't actually officiate at your wedding, but I'm happy to give you the same quality experience of premarriage counseling." I find that very cool!

Father James Martin's main message, which hit home with me, was that most Church leaders may not personally know someone who is LGBTQ+. They may know of them at a distance, but in terms of getting to know us—for example, by having dinner together—they lack that experience. James Martin writes that he fully understands why people like me would want to get away from that setting, but he basically says, "Look, unless you folks are involved in the Church in some way, its leaders, who sometimes come out with ignorant statements, will never have any real-world experience with who LGBTQ+ people are."

To me, this is similar to the way same-sex marriage in the United States grew to become a movement, state by state. Sociologists who studied how that trend happened explain that in the last ten years, many people actually got to know someone who is gay or lesbian. This is different from thirty or forty years ago, when most individuals did not know anybody who was openly LGBTQ+. Therefore, from what these social scientists say, if people have firsthand knowledge of our reality, the whole business of seeing us as evil beings who live under Satan's influence may fall away for many people. Given this context, James Martin suggests that in the same way, we could potentially transform the church. This empowering message truly resonated with me.

My Friend Became a Book

Martina Giselle Ramirez and Alicia Partnoy
July 13, 2018

A: We are already in the summer of 2018. Last summer around this time, we were at the hospital in Scottsdale, Arizona.

M: Hard to believe!

A: Right? This morning I remembered the day we were waiting to check out of the hotel. We were relaxing, just resting on our beds. You began telling me something fascinating, and I had to resist the impulse of getting up to grab the tape recorder . . .

M: What did I tell you?

A: I don't know! I thought it was an interesting way to end this book. Both of us after your surgery in that room, and me resisting the impulse of recording, thinking, "My friend is becoming a book. I don't want my friend to become a book!" I recall that you were telling me things you tell a friend, and there I was thinking about getting them on tape. There was stuff about your childhood, your relationship with your father, it was really interesting. But anyway, let's talk about happiness.

M: What about happiness?

A: See, all these popular magazines have articles about happiness. In the past they were all about sex, good orgasms, pleasing your man, and the like. Now they have lots of articles on happiness, joy, and how to live happy lives. For instance, if you look around at the supermarket checkout counter, *Time* magazine has a special issue on "The Science of Happiness." It's funny how we never expected this to happen when we chose a title for this book project. But let's do this again: on a scale from one to ten, how happy are you today?

M: Mhm, mhm.

A: You are not saying anything.

M: Oh, you're asking me! Oh, ok. How happy am I today? Certainly, it's better than when I used to just go home and have dinner and then sit in the dark because of my eyes. And I couldn't read books for months. That started to change in May. I went on that trip to the Bay Area to visit [my friend] Selene for five days, and

I was walking around with my hat and dark glasses. We went on six and seven-mile hikes when I suddenly realized that I didn't know I could do that! So here we are on these beaches or in sandy areas and, "Oh, I'm not terribly in pain." The eye always feels weird, but it didn't go into crazy pain. Then June came and I stopped wearing dark glasses at the computer. So I wondered, "Am I getting better at dealing with this, or is my condition improving?" Probably both, but I have been trying to avoid despair.

A: I know, I haven't asked you more about your heartbreak because I don't want you to cry.

M: I'm doing much better with all that. In the romance area I don't get close to people that way very often.

A: And today, on that scale of happiness, where are you?

M: There you go again! [*both laugh*] Well, the happiness went down again because I didn't get the dean job. Between messed up eyes, my breakup, and not getting the job that I really wanted, there was a period when I felt terrible. To be honest, I kept thinking that I was damaged goods. Was anybody going to want to be with me? People around me would say, "You're way more than just your eyes!" But I felt really low for a long time, thinking that if I had transitioned when I was younger, I'd have more of my own hair, I wouldn't have to wear wigs. But I lived many decades surrounded by all manner of high fences . . . In a way, I envy people that you see in publications like this one [*motioning to the summer issue of* Go *magazine*] because they live in such a different world. People with ten-year-old kids now might think, "Oh, my child is possibly transgender, let's try to make their path in life easier."

A: But do you realize that even when you envy their advantages in today's world, you are making their lives much more bearable by sharing your struggle?

M: Well, those of us born in my time come out of the dark ages. However, if we managed to make it through alive, we by default became examples of how life can be good after you transition.

The Journey Continues

Alicia Partnoy, October 17, 2018

Martina in a trailside mirror at Upper Newport Bay Nature Preserve, Newport Beach, California, June 2016

Dear Reader,

Gracias for walking with us through the past few years of Martina's journey in search of truth and happiness. We hope that this book helps you realize that you are not alone, gives you tools to learn about the struggles and victories of the LGBTQ+ community, and perhaps inspires you to put your own story down on paper. I would have liked more time to write some reflections, to share my journey from ignorance and prejudice to the path I walk today as an ally.

I would have loved to tell you more about María Eva Rossi, to whom we dedicate this book—about her struggle to be happy in my native town of Bahía Blanca, her yearning for a different world where love is not so elusive and social justice blesses us. I also wanted to share with you how María Eva's suicide in some way echoes my own brother's death. These and other reflections will have to wait. Life is happening with its urgencies, its demands, and this book is too necessary to be postponed.

Martina's story—as told here in her own voice, in our conversations, and in the writings and words of others touched by her life—is vital today. Martina's inspiration becomes crucial in a world where presidents, judges, clergymen, and the big farts who aim to rule forever over our minds, our bodies, and our homes, wish to take us back to the proverbial Middle Ages.

For decades, Cleis Press has asked me to publish a fourth book with them, a memoir. I have always replied that my memoir needs to be a collective work, since my life has been all about building a discourse of solidarity against oppression. This book is the closest to a memoir that I have produced. As I put the final touches to it, I know that on my desk and waiting for my attention are: a new poetry collection, a novel, an opera, a script for a play, and the theater adaptation by Deborah Merola of *The Little School* that will soon premiere in Nepal.

And on this October morning, as we finish this project, Martina is looking forward to completing applications for her dream job, one that fully utilizes her skills to impact institutions, and pays enough to keep supporting two homes—her former spouse's and hers. She also dreams of being outside again with her camera, immersed in nature, with no health issues limiting her joy. Martina talks frequently of her need for a simpler life, with time to make friends, and to find that precious jewel: a life partner with a generous heart, a bright mind, and a humble demeanor. Maybe this book will illuminate the path that leads to that amazing person too.

And the journey continues, dear reader. We are looking forward to meeting you in a bookstore, at a university auditorium, on social media, or at a demonstration. We know that we will keep on working together, walking together, weaving solidarities.

Los Angeles, LGBTQ+ History Month, 2018

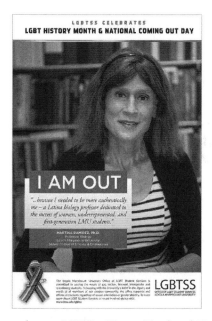

Martina as featured on an LGBTQ+ History Month and National Coming Out Day poster produced by Loyola Marymount University's Office of LGBT Student Services, October 2015. Photo by Richard Tamayo.

Postscript: 2019—The Year of Anniversaries

Martina Giselle Ramirez
March 16, 2019

Just after my recent birthday, I spent a week in Lima, Peru with a delegation of administrators and faculty drawn from the twenty-eight Jesuit colleges and universities in the United States. As I was unpacking and doing laundry last weekend at home, I happened to open a storage bin parked high on a shelf in my walk-in closet. Among other things, this bin contained a lingerie bag filled with a few padded bras from Victoria's Secret. A former Loyola Marymount University student gave me these bras shortly after I came out. As I held one of those bras again with a smile, it struck me how different my life is today compared to back then, and how 2019 will mark the attainment of a number of significant anniversaries. Specifically, it has been:

1. nine years since I came out at LMU and elsewhere
2. five years since I had my legal name changed, and

first had the "F" gender marker appear on legal documents

3. more than three years since I started living on my own

4. more than two years since my first gender-confirming surgery—vaginoplasty

5. almost two years since my second gender-confirming surgery—labiaplasty

My happier life as a woman can be seen in a now-versus-then comparison of where I live. For example, a walk through my two-room studio in Culver City shows some major changes compared with my room from nine years ago. Back then, my closet was largely filled with elements needed for my male-mode work "uniform" at LMU—polo shirts and khaki pants, a few jackets, and Oxfords, running shoes, and other "sensible" foot wear. Meanwhile, my dresser drawers were filled with underwear and socks in bland colors, as well as T-shirts, sweats, and old pants I used for working out, yard work, and spider collecting. My bathroom was quite Spartan, and when I slept, I looked out at bare walls.

Today, the contents of my walk-in closet and dresser are hugely different—the closet features a big shoe rack, which holds everything from flats to wedges; a regular dresser containing panties, bras, leggings, tights, and socks in multiples hues; and two hanger rods laden with dresses from maxis to above-the knee-styles, as well as tops of all sorts. And it's all in a blaze of colors. Around the corner is my bathroom, which is more packed than in the old days, including a Mac cosmetics organizer drawer parked next to the sink for ease of putting on foundation during the morning rush to work, as well as a tray of earrings. When a visitor comes to call, we can sit in my kitchen and share a meal and drinks, while gazing up at the many nature images that grace the walls. Or, we can move into my living room with its couch draped with colorful scarves as accents. My loft bed displays the community of stuffed animals I sleep with at night. In sum, I clearly live in a more colorful and pretty space than in the past, consistent with my happier outlook in 2019.

In this third month of 2019, there have also been some key developments compared with last year. For example, the eye problems noted earlier in this book *may* be on the road to some degree of improvement. Specifically, since November 2018, greater portions of my day have featured less blur, though the left eye still tends to be blurrier. The other milestone is that I stopped using dark glasses when outdoors in early February 2019. I still wear a hat or hold an unfurled umbrella over my head to shield the right eye from direct sunlight—but while it still reacts, it does not "go over the edge" in terms of pain as it did before, and mostly recovers once I move indoors.

Since I was concerned that spending more than a year behind dark glasses might lead me to lose what tolerance I had for light, I decided one day to see what would happen if I went back to not wearing them—and then I never retreated. While I still use yellow-tinted dark glasses for driving at night, given the over-the-top brightness of many auto headlights in Los Angeles, being able to see the colors of the natural world once again, unmediated by darkened plastic, is huge for me as a nature photographer. Of course, especially for aging eyes, there are some good reasons to use dark glasses, but for now, I need to try to get back to the light tolerance I used to have before, and then go from there.

The other surprising development is how much more attuned I am to womanly beauty, and thus I find myself getting attracted and turned on when I encounter certain women. Perhaps that's because I'm single and looking, but in any case, I was never that way before—women caught my eye first and foremost because of who they were (that is, were they big hearted and kind?), and their physical features were not a big deal. So this "physical first" reaction—which I first noticed last summer—is something I had no idea was coming. Indeed, one of my good friends now jokes about my list of "crushes," since she has spent months listening to me periodically wander into her office to share news of who just appeared on my radar screen. Still, with such individuals, unless I sense qualities of goodness, they won't qualify as people who are life partner candidates for me.

Thus, 2019 finds me in a much better space than nine years ago, though still with that striving for the better—for the "more" that led me to come out in the first place. And so, as I look to the road ahead, it's with the spirit of Ulysses—"To strive, to seek, to find, and not to yield,"—and with the hope of perhaps finding a life partner who will accept me as I am and stick with me no matter what.

Martina on her birthday, February 2019

9   Jorgensen and Stryker, *Christine Jorgensen,* 111.

10   Jorgensen and Stryker, *Christine Jorgensen,* 144.

11   Jorgensen and Stryker, *Christine Jorgensen,* 164-165.

12   Jorgensen and Stryker, *Christine Jorgensen,* 307.

13   Jorgensen and Stryker, *Christine Jorgensen, 217.*

14   David G. Savage, "Supreme Court Grants Emergency Order to Block Transgender Male Student in Virginia from Using Boys' Restroom," *Los Angeles Times,* August 3, 2016. https://www.latimes.com/nation/la-na-court-transgender-20160803-snap-story.html

15   The Gallup-Purdue Index Report. *Great jobs, great lives: A study of more than 30,000 college graduates across the U.S.* (2014)

16   Father Gregory Boyle (@FrGregBoyle), "Imagine a circle of compassion with nobody standing outside that circle." September 8, 2015, 5:11 p.m., https://twitter.com/frgregboyle/status/641358218388639745?lang=en

17   German Lopez summarizes its effect, "It overturned and banned local statutes that protect LGBTQ+ people from discrimination based on sexual orientation or gender identity. And it prohibited transgender people from using bathrooms and locker rooms that align with their gender identity in schools and government buildings . . . " German Lopez. HB2, North Carolina's sweeping anti-LGBTQ+ law, explained." *Vox,* March 20, 2017. https://www.vox.com/2016/2/23/11100552/charlotte-north-carolina-lgbtq-pat-mccrory

18   Kenneth Oldfield, "Humble and Hopeful: Welcoming First-Generation Poor and Working-Class Students to College," *About Campus* 11, no. 6 (Jan–Feb 2017): 2-12.

19   Clark Kerr, cited by Peggy Hawley. *Being Bright is Not Enough: The Unwritten Rules of Doctoral Study. Third Edition.* (Springfield: Charles C. Thomas, Publisher, 2010), 29

20   Ernest Boyer. *College: The Undergraduate Experience in America.* (New York: Harper & Row, 1987). 11.

21   Julia L. Aaker, Avery Baird, James W. Cahalan, Fatima Omar, Kylie E. Swanson, and Siri Thompson, "Approaching the Transi-

Notes

1   Eli Green, "A Toolkit for Becoming a Transgender Ally," Filmed April 17, 2016 at TEDxYouth@SanDiego in San Diego, CA, video, 9:18, https://www.youtube.com/watch?v=Of-DG31_Z4w.

2   Janet Mock, *Redefining Realness: My Path to Womanhood, Identity, Love, and So Much More* (New York: Atria Books, 2014).

3   Susan Faludi, *In the Darkroom* (New York: Metropolitan Books, 2016).

4   Mariette Pathy Allen, *The Gender Frontier* (Heidelberg: Kehrer, 2003).

5   Start Making Sense and Jon Weiner, "Mourn. Resist. Organize. These Are Our Tasks Now," *The Nation*, November 10, 2016. https://www.thenation.com/article/mourn-resist-organize-these -are-our-tasks-now.

6   Please see previous chapter.

7   Christine Jorgensen and Susan Stryker, *Christine Jorgensen: A Personal Autobiography* (Jersey City: Cleis, 2000).

8   Jorgensen and Stryker, *Christine Jorgensen*, 99.

tion to Adulthood: Vocational and Career Discernment Among Undergraduates." Meeting of the Midwest Sociological Society, March 11, 2011.

22   Martina Ramirez and Laura Fandino, "Genetic Variability and Gene Flow in *Metepeira ventura (Araneae, Araneidae)." Journal of Arachnology* 24, no. 24 (1996): 1-8.

23   Martina Ramirez, B. Cashin, Jr., L. Ponce, B. Chi, and Pam Lum, *"Genetic Diversity Among Island and Mainland Populations of the California Trapdoor Spider Bothriocyrtum californicum (Araneae, Ctenizidae),"* Arachnology, 16, no. 1 (2013): 1-9.

24   Mock, *Redefining Realness,* 230.